IN AWE OF IT ALL

STORIES AND INSPIRATIONS
from a Spiritual Journey through
Eight Decades of Life on This Earth

Sherry Dee Lady

Photography by Julie Lady Hall

LUMINARE PRESS
WWW.LUMINAREPRESS.COM

Dan,
Best to you on
your journey —
it's a wonderful
life — enjoy it all.
Sherry Dee Lady

Luminare Press
442 Charnelton St.
Eugene, OR 97401
www.luminarepress.com

LCCN: 2021911323
ISBN: 978-1-64388-669-5

Dedicated with much love and appreciation to:

My beautiful, incredible children,
Julie and Jeff, and their father Robert

My amazing sister, Kathleen

My beloved spiritual community, Unity of the Valley

And to Alan, my teacher, inspiration
and special friend

Special thank you also to Jon, my ministerial
colleague, for his expert editing for our
newsletter all those years.

TABLE OF CONTENTS

COMMUNICATING

PARTICIPATING

INTEGRATING

RADIATING

ANTICIPATING

APPRECIATING

CELEBRATING

Communicating

―∞―

*"Above all else guard your heart for
everything you do flows from it."*

—Proverbs 4:23

*"Before you speak, let your words pass through these gates:
Is it true? Is it necessary? Is it kind? Will it hurt anyone?
Will it improve on the silence?"*

—Satya Sai Baba

FRIENDSHIP

While watching an old fashioned VHS tape the other day that showed clips from past TV sitcoms, a song from one of the shows got stuck in my mind and is still sitting there replaying itself over and over. That might have happened to some of you somewhere along the way as well. The song was from the sitcom "Laverne and Shirley" and the words are stuck in my brain are:

"Friendship, friendship, such a perfect blend-ship. When other friendships have been forgot, ours will still be hot."

The word "hot" did not mean then what it means today. Back then it meant really warm, cozy, special, alive, etc. It some instances it could possibly have meant a "hot romance," but since this was describing a special friendship between two roommates who were sharing life, work, and adventures in interacting with the world, it meant the other warm, sharing kind. It reminded me of my first year of teaching when I lived with a college friend here in Eugene. While we taught at different schools, it was a year of sharing not only living space and some outside activities, but also preparations for upcoming weddings for each of us the following summer. The friendship required blending of different personalities and lives, and that experience has meant so much through the years at many different times.

The word that appeals to me is "blend-ship". I think about the many friends I have made through the years and while good connections, not all were of a closer connection that I would describe as a "perfect blend-ship," though some were. My closest friend from high school days passed away a few months ago and I really miss staying in touch with her. We lived miles apart, but there is a saying that relates to our connection: "True friends are never apart. Maybe in distance, but not in the heart."

These days of separation through pandemic isolation and quarantine, have altered the ways we interact with friends and that has been very difficult for many of us. While some connections have faded to a degree, others have become highlighted and brought closer and affirmed our place in this life together. On the days when I feel sort of at loose ends, down and out, or even confused, it has been a blessing to have been able to stay connected in various ways with those who have been willing to stay close in heart with me. The blessing of a special supportive, willingly interactive and trusted friend has brought a silver lining to any clouds of doubt or hopelessness I have felt and that often fills the spaces left by others. My prayer for you is that you have at least one special friend in your life, and enough others that have been willing to stay close in heart with you, as well. If not, then be courageous and reach out and find someone who would probably love to hear from you. It often takes just one special friend to bring the glorious sunshine of life back into being for each other.

Along the way, we can also know that we have an expert, experienced and willing silver-cloud liner in the Holy Spirit of Love and Life that created us, that wants to be there for us, cares about us, that asks to be called upon and graciously listens while affirming us and providing for our needs. We can find that Spirit sand let it breathe life into us through our daily prayers, meditations, quiet times, and yes, even in our time of begging and beseeching, and calling for relief—what has often been referred to as "on our knees" both physically and in the heart. Our present very special spiritual community continue to offer guidance for connection and finding peace within. No distance, never apart and always in the heart.

As I conclude this essay I hear the rapid footsteps of the adorable squirrel that like to scamper across the beams of my deck fence. I hear the thump of the large black bird as it lands on my float roof and begins to peck noisily away at something up there that I have yet to determine its identity. I toss out various seeds for them, but not up that high. I also hear the bark of a dog and see my neighbor talking hers for a walk. Now I want to hear the laughter of the children next door out in their yard, but it is still too cold for that. So, in longing for some kind of connection, I will put on my comfy Nikes, get into my car and with the blue sky and sun to accompany me, I will head for my beloved park where the trees are shedding their leaves very rapidly, people are either walking or jogging, children sometimes playing, and where, if a tear needs to fall, it can be dried quickly by an autumn breeze. I am so grateful for this park and all it continues to offer me spiritually. I am very happy there and after a visit, peace is once more restored to my life.

Oh my, how grateful am I for this life, for all of my friends, for this day. May you know that feeling, too.

In my often unseen and virus-distanced way, I am here for and with you. May we have a continued "perfect blend-ship."

Love,

Sherry

HOW TO BE
A SUPER STAR

A spectacular and rare "Christmas Star" is coming. If you managed to see the crescent Moon pass Jupiter and Saturn this week, you will have noticed something else. They are now really, really close to each other, and on December 21, the date of the December Solstice, they are going to almost appear to collide to become one super bright point of light. They will look like a double planet for the first time since the year 1226. Close to 800 years ago. Some say that such a "star" happens about every 800 years. If you calculate 800 years before 1226 that would put the star appearing around 426 A.D.

In reality, Jupiter and Saturn will be millions of miles apart, not close at all by our measurements, but celestially it will be close enough to look like one bright star. I find that rather exciting and phenomenal in its own way because alignments between those two planets are so rare. It is thought by some astronomers that the "star of Bethlehem" was a rare triple conjunction of Jupiter, Saturn and Venus. I am hoping for clear skies so I can see that "star" and let it teach me what is has, and wants to teach me, which I believe is significant on the spiritual level if we open to it.

Jesus was reported to have said, "You are the Light of the world" and then told us to not hide our Light under a bushel, but to let it shine for others. Let it shine not just to light a pathway or a dark corner, but to illuminate the world around us. And so we pray, meditate, affirm that God/Spirit lives within us, practice the principles as we know them, learn about loving our neighbor as best we can, etc. and then we walk into a world filled with chaos, viruses, division, confusion, and disparity and the light we hold in the sky of our daily lives without and within, begin to dim in spite of our efforts to keep it going. It's not "bad"—it's just something that happens sometimes.

Then in the midst of it all, comes Christmas. Christmas in a COVID lock-down that finds us scattered from all we knew the season to be a time when we joined our lights with others in celebration of the birth of the new kind of Love brought down through the ages. The light can potentially begin to fade—until we remember what is still within our reach. EACH OTHER!

It took two planets, and on one occasion a rare three planet coming-together to create a light called "a Star," shining brightly in the heavens. We can create our own Christmas star and fill our life heavens, inner and outer, with so much light that this time in the history of our world and our lives, will be talked about centuries down the line as the time when human kind, and all life forms, lifted their hearts, minds, and spirits to new heights of magnificence because they believed in, cared for, loved, and created a miracle on earth like never before seen.

It only takes a phone call, a text message, a card in the mail, a virtual hug…any acknowledgement of another's presence in our lives to keep the brightness going like an eternal flame, making our personal and collective heavens lit up like the sky of long ago, and maybe even brighter.

What one planet could not do alone, two or three accomplished by allowing the laws of the universe to flow naturally. These laws govern us as well and the star of our being is there to guide us if we allow it.

Become the SUPER STAR that you are. Reach out and glow with heavenly light as you take the hand of someone—anyone—who comes to your mind or into your daily experience. Glory on the highest!! Peace on earth.

Love,

Sherry

A WALK IN
THE WOODS

L ike many of you, once I fully realized that I was, indeed, going to spending most of my days indoors I started paying attention to some of the things I have put off for a long time. One of them was going through bookshelves, thinking I would have the courage to release some of them and create more space for—probably more books as is my passion. Do any of you have this tendency to collect books? More than could be possibly read in a lifetime?

During the process I came across one of my favorite books…"A Walk In the Woods: Meditations on Mindfulness with a Bear named Pooh" by Dr. Joseph Parent and Nancy Parent. Upon randomly opening to whatever place wanted to be noticed, I came across these words that I am delighted to share with you:

"As he stepped outside, Pooh felt the soft moist moss under his feet. He smelled the rich sweetness of the honeysuckle (his favorite flower of course) on the climbing vines curling around the tree…He heard the birds singing and the wind whistling (Or were the birds whistling and the wind singing?)… Here were the trees, bushes, hills, dales, creeks and ponds that made up the Hundred Acre Wood.

Now it was time for his daily exercises (said Pooh).

Pooh raised his chubby little arms high in the air, or at least as high as they would go. He could feel the pull along his arms and shoulders and sides. Then he bent over to touch his toes—or at least as far as he could reach down to them. He could feel the stretch in the back of his legs.

He did this movement exactly seven times—not six, nor eight, Then he walked slowly and mindfully to the big log in front of his house, his Not-Thinking Spot…He sat up straight so he could take nice, full breaths, drew air into his nose…then breathed out. The rhythm of his breath—filling and emptying—lulled him into a comfortable calm.

As he rested there, deeply grounded and firmly centered in his Not-Thinking-Spot, Pooh felt at peace.

After appreciating his environment, doing exercises, and practicing mindfulness of breathing, Pooh knew that his body and mind were as ready as they could be for whatever the day might bring."

It goes on to say that after Pooh did this "work," he then went on to his practicing kindness routine. He did this by gathering his warm thoughts and sending them out into the world, as well as carrying them with him in case he met someone on his walks that he wanted to share them with, while affirming: "Today I'll be the Best Friend I can be, to everyone I see, including me."

Some wonderful, gentle, reminders for putting into and filling our strange days. These from a fictional character— though he is very much alive to me since I adore and collect teddy bears. Yes, I even have a large teddy bear on the front seat of my car. His name is Spencer and he is there, not just in place of a missing friend, but as an object of communication and comfort for me. He does have to sit in the back if someone gets in my car, unless they are willing to hold him.

Back to Pooh—and our lives today. What can I say? Except that this is not an easy time for me—nor for you. Pooh and I offer this well-known saying:

"The Past is History, the Future's a Mystery
Being Here and Now is a Precious Gift,
That's why we call it The Present."

ENJOY THE JOURNEY

A couple of amusing quotes have been drifting around on the internet and Facebook lately and they have brought me to a halt in the middle of very busy days more than once. The halting has been a good thing for me in those busy moments because they slowed me down long enough to get a good chuckle and pass them on to friends to hopefully lighten their day as well.

I want to share a couple of the quotes with you and though you may be familiar with them, maybe they will still provide more thoughts and a chuckle or two.

First saying: "Life's journey is not to arrive at the grave safely in a well preserved body, but rather to skid in sideways, totally worn out, and shouting 'Holy cow—what a ride." The idea of being "totally worn out" does not appeal to me, because I seem to reach that stage a little more easily now and I want to preserve enough energy to do some of the fun things that are still available to me while I still have the energy. (I wouldn't mind having the naturally well preserved body to finish the ride with however).

The theme of that sentence is one that appeals to me though. There are so many wonderful things available to us that can enhance and supplement the daily routines of our lives, yet so often they get put "on the back burner" and when we try to bring them to the front burner, we can't, as one sweet friend shared with me " even find the stove we set them on because we gave it away a long time ago and forgot to keep the pot of dreams accessible." Or as another friend shared "I sometimes feel like I am on a fast moving train and out the window I can see things I've always wanted to see and do being passed by, or being done by others, while I just sit here and wonder what went wrong? Why aren't I doing some of those things?" So what is keeping us from sliding into the next experience, a bit breathless, and shouting to the world that it was truly an amazing ride? I'll let you think on that for a while. There's still time to change that if you want to.

Second saying: "When I get older and my hair turns gray, I don't want people to say " there goes a sweet old lady'. I want them to say "What the heck is she up to now?" My daughter said she has been telling her friends through the years all the things I was "up to" and they were always amazed. Really? I liked her saying that, because sometimes I think I've left so much undone and not yet experienced—so I put that quote above my computer to remind me. There are so many things yet to "be up to." I guess some people call it a "bucket list," but buckets, to me, have limits as to how much one can put into them. So I write things I'd like to do on sticky notes, put them into a notebook and when I've done them I write a note about the experience. All will go into my "not a best seller" autobiography that I will leave for my grandchildren. If something becomes impossible to do—like I have to give up the thought of climbing up a mountain in Tibet now—I can just remove the sticky note, bless it and know I have had mountain-top experiences in other ways, and some just recently, which have brought so much happiness into my life.

So if you want to, go ahead and be sweet old ladies, or old men, if you want to, and know You will be loved and admired by me no matter what; but, don't forget to also make the most of every second you have left in this lifetime and let yourself be blessed by the courage to step out anew each day to find enjoyment along the way. Then you and I can slide into the next life safely, but with a big smile on our faces, knowing it was indeed, a wonderful ride!

A silly poem I wrote for you, at the beach, on a sunny day not too long ago.

> Higgles and sniggles and riffles go all the
> way up to my nose
> While giggles, and wiggles and piggles go
> all the way down to my toes.
> And—happles, and snapples and rapples
> extend beyond ear tops and lobes.
> I can't help but feeling emotals,
> Upon this biggelty day,
> For sunnies and bunnies and funnies
> Have tickled me into praise,
> For the waffles and toffles and loffles of life
> That embrace me in powerful ways…
> May laffies, and sweetlies, and nothing but
> joytles
> Be present in each of your heart-iest days.

A LESSON WELL
LEARNED

I learned an important life lesson when I was 8 or 9—the actual age eludes me, probably because this isn't about my being young, old, or somewhere in between. It's about a lesson not unlike most learning experiences which we set aside until something really big comes along to remind us that we have something in our consciousness that was planted long ago in case we needed to use it.

Anyway, "back then" I was given a packet of seeds from an elderly neighbor whose rather shamble-like, all wooden, shake-sided house bordered our farm. He told me that there were three kinds of seeds in the packet, but he was not going to tell me what they were. I was to plant them in 10-inch pots and wait until they grew and bloomed and then see how they turned out. He said I was to water them daily and keep them in full sunlight until their flowers appeared.

I did as he said, until the day when their flowers appeared. Two beautiful red flowers appeared on one stem, five yellow ones on another, but the third just showed rather unattractive, gray-green leaves on a somewhat prickly stalk. I was not impressed with that one at all, but I took care of it anyway. On one of the days when the neighbor came to check his "experiment" as he called it, I complained about the not-so-pretty plant. I said I did not really want to keep that one anymore because there were no flowers on it. He told me I would just have to wait a bit longer so the experiment could be completed. So for another 10 days or so, I looked at it only on occasion and I watered it a bit less than the others sort of hoping it would give up so I could use the pot for another plant.

Then one morning, having decided to set the barren plant in a separate place and keep the other two plants together, I saw it—a deeply purple flower on the top of the prickly stem. I couldn't believe it, as the purple was such a rich color. And it had grown a little taller than the other two just over night. After getting permission, I began running to our neighbor's house and then saw him coming my way. "It's blooming!" I shouted. He replied, "I knew it would, sooner or later." And then, as we reached the plants and he said "good morning" to them (he was rather weird to me at that age), and he told me that his experiment was a success and that he hoped I would understand.

"You see," he said. "Plants are our teachers. In this experiment you did what people usually do. They ooh and aah over the plants that look the loveliest and ignore the other one. Yet, it is the one that, despite its tiny flowers, offers us powerful medicine when we know how to extract and use it. Scientists and doctors know all about this plant. You will notice how strong and tall it stands in the sun? That's because it has a special mission and it knows it."

We are like this plant in many ways. Sometimes we think we have nothing to offer and we hide away our special gifts deep inside. When we see other people becoming like a brilliant flower, we think we can't ever be that way as well. It's our thoughts that keep us from blooming, but in truth, when we push those thoughts aside and not believe them, no matter how often they show up, we can free ourselves, deep inside, to open a space for our beautiful flower to come forth for all to see. We can choose to let the beauty of what we are inside become the rays of love and peace that can transform not only ourselves into the magnificent being we were meant to be, but we can also share that in such a way that others can do the same, become the same and have a magnificent life as well. It takes patience and practice and vigilance, but the result is worth it. Don't let anyone tell you that you aren't beautiful and don't let yourself say it to you either.

A TRUE CONFESSION

Rain on my roof sounds like rain on a rustic cabin in the woods and when I experience the sound I find myself soothed, relaxed and feeling very cozy. On a recent rainy day, however, I was anything but calm and found myself yelling into the landline phone on my desk and repeatedly punching the O(zero) button with the determination to eventually get a live voice that could answer my question and give me some guidance. When the voice finally came onto the line, I asked my question in louder than usual volume, and was told to take care of the business by going to my computer and logging in to my account. Maybe some of you have experienced this? (If so, I hope you responded better than I did.)

I very firmly replied, in my firm and louder than normal voice, "I have tried this but it didn't work. I will try it again, but I want you to stay on the line and help me walk through this. Do you understand?" "But ma'am all you have to do is......" I said, I need you to stay on the line until the transaction is completed, because I don't know how to answer some of the questions and your company was the one responsible for putting me in this position by giving incorrect directions. Are you still there?" "Yes, Ma'am." "Good and don't you dare leave until this is taken care of." All said with my most demanding and firm voice, my heart pounding, and my feet curled tensely on the floor.

Obviously, I was getting out of control, and I knew it, but in that moment I didn't care, because it had taken me two months and a lot of paperwork and in person conversations to get to this point. The voice, sounding a little terrified, stuck with me until the task was completed (about 10 minutes) and as I typed in the last dollar sign and period, I finally relaxed enough to realize I was not only out of control, but also very rude. I tried to fix it by calling again and speaking kindly to the voice. I even asked for a name and where could I send a letter of commendation on the now to be named person's behalf. In the middle of my offer I heard "Thank you for choosing our company" followed by the click of the phone. "Good grief, Sherry," I actually said out loud, "you may think you deserve an Oscar, but you really deserve a good kick in the pants."

Sometimes life forces us into positions where we can either walk appropriately through them without elevated blood pressure, or we can become drama queens—or kings—and forget all about those spiritual-behavioral principles we have been taught and want to practice; only to realize we have, once again, fallen off our own expectation pedestal. Asking forgiveness for self and others is a good thing to do at this point while we remember that people who experience success in life may fall out of practice, but pick themselves up again and continue where they left off and just get going again. How do we do that? Here are some things I have found that help, and hopefully you will as well, though none of them are new. We just need to keep them in our tool box for those most "dramatic" times in our lives.

1. Take a deep breath and practice deep breathing often.

2. Be mindful by staying more fully in the present with awareness of our potential for peaceful living.

3. Be grateful for even the small things and successes and the presence of the Divine in all things.

4. Keep daily practices that include times in silence and/or meditation.

5. Move, exercise, play, laugh and nourish the physical body.

6. Build support systems that are there in the bumpy times, and in times of joy.

7. Continually work on how we think about things. Thoughts held in mind produce after their kind.

8. Take time to smell the roses (old adage).

9. Say to yourself "It's ok. I can and will get better." And get back to your life. Apologize, even if you don't quite feel like it yet. Do it with a smile and see what comes back to you.

Heading off now to be in the silence, so I can realign my whole life if it is needed; and to connect with that beautiful Holy Spirit that understands, accepts, forgives, and fills each cell with Divine love, joy and gratitude while nudging us ever forward into the peace that is possible and which passes all understanding.

A BUMPY, GRUMPY
ROAD TO JOY

"In order to find that internal place of joy, it is important to embrace all parts of ourselves, all parts of our experience."

—Lorena Smith

"Life is simple. Everything happens for you, not to you."

—Byron Katie

Oh my, how I would have fumed, and fought and argued 40+ years ago (or even earlier in my life) about those two statements. "Easy for you to say!" would have been one response. Another might have been, "Yeah, right! A lot you don't know about life, looks like." Or maybe "Things can be good, really good, but as soon as it gets too good you can be sure something *not* good will come along. So enjoy the good but don't expect it to stick around." Any of you ever felt that way? Like the old saying, "Just sitting here waiting for the other shoe to drop," that some older people in my family used to share, especially the farmers who depended on the success of their crops for everything.

In spite of a pretty happy and successful life, I just couldn't buy into the "happy, happy, happy" every second attitude with what I thought was a hidden agenda full of buried and stuffed down feelings that sticky sweet smiles could not fully hide, though I was "guilty" of appearing to have the same buy-in to how you should show up in the world. I used to envy the characters on sitcoms who, through a cleverly written script, could let it all hang out, say it like it is and then get a good laugh from the audience.

In other words, it was easier to put down the "cherubic cheerfuls" than it was to look at why I didn't feel that way. I wouldn't allow myself to discover what was truly in the way of my saying "yes" to all aspects of life; embracing, accepting, appreciating, and acknowledging the place within me that kept singing but that I didn't let show very often.

So what changed? Why was I able to say to a friend one day—when we were traveling to one of our retreats together and she was wearing her sweatshirt with the word JOY on the front—"You know it is so good to feel joy no matter what happens, isn't it? Deep down joy, even when you are crying or yelling at the world about something." To which she replied, "Yup. Who would have 'thunk it." In all honesty, we both agreed that Joy had made a difference in our lives. The inspirational literature we were reading, the marvelous people we're meeting, the great speakers we heard as a result of attending anything on spiritual living that was offered within a reasonable geographic area (or at least reachable by plane)…and the realization that in the beginning of our lives we had been given the freedom to be ourselves and the promise of internal joy when we live from knowing that we are good and holy just the way we are. Byron Katie's statement that "Everything happens at exactly the right moment, neither too soon or too late," was now operational for both of us. As the ancient and wise saying reminds me, the student was ready and the teacher appeared. Byron Katie also said, "You don't have to like it, it's just easier if you do." So much easier, yes—and so much joy in the middle of everything. Spirit knows what is best for us. It just takes a long time to get there sometimes.

Do I still Grinch once in a while? Yes. Plenty of people can attest to that. I'm only human. But when it is verbalized, it often gets a laugh (unplanned on my part). Maybe it happens because while I'm letting out the "dust bunnies of thought," I'm also laughing at how silly I am and how joyful I feel in spite of it all.

WHAT DO YOU VALUE?

M onday, January 20th we, as a nation, will celebrate the life of Martin Luther Jr.—our radical human rights revolutionary, our American Gandhi, who had a dream and shared it with not only "us," but the world as a whole through his words and deeds. Until he was violently removed from our presence, he never wavered from his goal of challenging the values being expressed in our country burning those years in the late 1960s. So much has been written about him and his quest for change in our understanding and expression of human rights, not just for what has been referred to as "his people," but for all people everywhere. These statements from one of his speeches caught my interest.

"If we are going to get on the right side of the world…we as a nation must undergo a radical revolution of values. We must rapidly begin the shift from a thing-oriented society to a person-oriented society…There is nothing to prevent us from reordering our priorities so that the pursuit of peace will take precedence over the pursuit of war." MLK, NYC, 1967. He then share what he values: Equality, Faith, Nonviolence, Education, Love, Leadership, and Selflessness.

I have recently been involved in conversations with friends about what we have come to value over the years of our lives. We agreed that though our basic values have not changed, many very meaningful ones have been added as we have journeyed through Earth School. One set of values expressed by a good friend, who is also one of our congregants, was especially meaningful because of the inclusion of so many expansive things. With his permission, I share these with you. No doubt you will have some of your own, as well.

Alan Reeder Values:

- Love, Love, Love and Respect
- Integrity and Honoring the Truth
- Beauty and Uniqueness
- Inclusion and Honoring Differences
- Community and Belonging
- Humor, Playfulness and Friendliness
- Peace—"Peace is my Middle Name"
- Worship and Contemplation
- Learning, Imagination and Creativity
- Spiritual Exploration
- Prayer and Meditation
- Companionship, Commitment and Being Sentimental
- Family and Friends
- Being Productive and Wise

- Healing and Forgiveness

- Letting Go

- Patience and Hope

- Gratitude and Positive Thinking

- Service, Support, Helping and Sharing

- Joy and Happiness

And—Valuing the Sacredness of all Life

"What we Think, Feel, Believe and Want determines much of what we experience."

—A.R. 1/20

The act of writing down the things I value—including everything on Alan's list, which will no doubt continue to expand—has made me also aware of many other little things in each and every day that may not be "list-worthy" but have become shining valued moments in my thoughts.

For example: I value the mind that created drive-up mailbox drops so I don't have to get out of the car in the rain; the person who pumps my gas and always smiles, my traveling teddy bear because he is such a good non-judgmental listener. I also have come to value what may seem like silly things perhaps—toothpaste in a tube because I grew up having to use baking soda and salt and did not like it; fish oil in capsules so I don't have to take cod-liver oil by spoon; my neighbor's cat because it stops by to check on me almost every day. I have said to these things out loud (but softly): "Toothpaste tune, by golly I value you… Mailbox, I appreciate your position in life, etc." I have become a constant user of the word "value" and it has been such fun, especially when I remember to tell other people how much they are valued.

The list made by our mutual congregant-friend includes things of Heart, Mind, Soul and Spirit, all of which, when acknowledged, and held with Love and Respect, can make such a difference in our lives and the lives of others. When we live from these values, then who we are, what we do and how we respond can bring about the peaceful revolution so longed for by us all. What would you add to the list? What do you value deep in your heart?

I value you—more than you may know. Thank you for being here, with me, at this time in my life and in our spiritual community.

IT'S ALL ABOUT BANANA BREAD—REALLY!

A friend brought me two nice thick slices of freshly baked banana bread as a contribution to our lunch and, as was stated, in appreciation for being able to have a quiet lunch in my home. When the meal was over, I popped my piece into the toaster as she looked on in disbelief. "Why are you doing that?" she asked. "It's fresh. I just made it this morning." "I know," I replied. That's why I toast it. I prefer my breads less moist and a bit crispy around the edges when warmed." She didn't understand, may have been a bit offended though she hid it well, and it was obvious she had never heard of doing that.

What ensued was a whole discussion about foods we liked and didn't like—things like really spicy and not spicy, sweet versus salty, vegan versus traditional, raw vs cooked, and a lot of other things—all of which had us almost doubled over with laughter after a while. Then we went on to TV shows, fashions, vacations, and lots of other things. We ended up marveling about how little we knew on the level of likes and dislikes even after a good many years of friendship dating back to high school days. (For me that's a long way back, as some of you may know).

As time passed on that day, we got down to some pretty serious and basic things and had we not been friends for so long, we might have ended up being a bit hesitant to agreeing to a next time for lunch, had it not been for being able to come to the realization that on one basic level there was no doubt we were in agreement: our basic internal spiritual understandings. She worships in a more traditional church, while I am, according to her, "really, really open minded." This is hard for her sometimes she said, because it means you have to be open to everything, which is not the general tenure of her expressions. Because of the realization we came to, we were able to move on to the more serious business of taking hold of the opportunity to build new bridges of understanding and acceptance.

We were in agreement on five things: 1) there is only One Power in the universe and we honor that, 2) we need to let go of stereotypes and racial biases since it has been proven scientifically that we all came from one basic racial color with adaptations along the way, and 3) love and acceptance and a chance to live fruitful lives is a common heartfelt wish of all peoples everywhere, as well as a deep human need, 4) because of all the upheaval in all corners and structures in the world today, we need to recognize our oneness and act from that place so we can be there for each other and 5) Forgiveness and love are keys to correcting all misunderstandings and crucial to human growth, survival and evolvement.

"Let's see," she said, as she was preparing to leave, "this has been the most fun we have ever had together and it all started out with banana bread—crispy edges or not crispy edges. Who would have thought the lowly banana could have such powers within it to spark this kind of discussion." I agreed. We hugged. A week later she sent a new recipe for cauliflower bread, with the message: "Well, the fruit world got it's acknowledgement. Let's see what the veggie world can do. You bake it, toast your part for the crispy edges, and let's get together again soon." We will—after Christmas though as she is on her way to California for a while.

Maybe it's in the getting older that people are able to put aside other things and get down to the essences of good friendships; or maybe it's because in this time of transition, only the things that are true and honest and real and from the heart have to come forth so we can save ourselves from the fallout of personal and planetary chaos and go on to build a better world for all.

I will never see banana bread quite the same way again—but I will always see you as my perfect partners on this path we are sharing. Thank you for who you are—crusty edges or not. Either way is perfect.

PEACE, HARMONY AND— ARE YOU SURE OF THAT?

When I was in the middle of my teaching career, I was the person responsible one year for a classroom of thirty one fifth grade students who taught me more about life than any other group I have ever known, before or since. Those beautiful, brilliant, beguiling and often bewildering human beings knew more about the universe, how it works, and what it requires of us than I could have imagined. Here's an example:

Mahatma Gandhi wisely said "Happiness is when what you think, what you say and what you do are in harmony". I liked this so much that I had it done in calligraphy and put in the center of my personal teacher's small bulletin board behind my desk. The literal truth of this was tested one day when—I'll call him Sam—came stomping up to my desk, took the math paper he held in his hand and tore it into pieces, put them on my desk and walked away with a smug look on his face while chanting "I hate math" several times. He was truly not feeling in harmony with math in that moment. I decided to check it out.

I asked Sam to come back to my desk, sit down on the "talking with Mrs. Lady chair"—and tell me about what I just witnessed. He pointed to the sign behind my desk. "Just like the sign says… I agree with what I thought, and what I said and what I did and now I'm happy. Is there a problem with that?" I couldn't think of one. Except that there was now an incomplete math assignment, and my uncertainty about what to do with a literal interpretation of words poetically strung together on the subject of harmony.

It made me think of another quote by a man named Doug Floyd—"You don't get harmony when everyone sings the same note." Sam was not singing the same note as either Gandhi or me, though like Sam, I have a love-hate relationship with math and understand the frustration. So, in essence, singing different notes can bring about harmony—if they are not of a dissonant nature, or maybe if they are in reality it's because everything in the world is orchestrated through a gradual process with the goal to be the establishment of harmony through integration, confluence, shared values, common purpose, fluid movement, etc. and that takes time.

Carl Sagan, famous scientist, told us that "the universe is not required to be in perfect harmony with human ambition. Success is to be in harmony with existence, to be always calm and to always let each wave of life wash us a little farther up shore." As a teacher I was a little "farther up shore" than Sam, but Sam was in process of being washed a little farther up the shore of youth-to-adult, and it was my job to not inhibit the process with anger, but to bring into the situation some tender, accepting and peaceful moments so that grappling with math could bring about some balance between mind, body and soul.

Harmony, like the progression of music by its individual notes can be achieved through the realization that "we are different instruments, playing our own melody, each one tuned to a different key…coming together in harmony." (from Unity hymn "Weave Us Together"). In this way we can re-establish the original harmony that once existed between us and the universe. That is so needed right now, this moment, and it is our responsibility and privilege, to assist our future generation in "meaning what you say, but not saying it meanly" and bringing about happiness on a new and profound level so peace and harmony may be a reality while bringing about healing and wholeness for all as we overcome the challenges of living in today's world.

ONE STEP AT A TIME

I t's too big. There are too many people and too many problems. There's too much going on. Everything seems to be falling apart. The whole world is a big mess and I don't know how to fix any part of it. I can't seem to make even the slightest difference that will last. I don't know who to help first. How do we sort it out?

These are comments offered at a small group discussion in which I recently became involved at a local coffee shop. I was introduced as a "pastor" by one of the people in the group and after we shared some usual conversation one person asked me what advice I could give them from my "perspective". What people often don't realize is that being a minister does not mean I don' t also get confused about some of the world's problems or think I have some solutions to it all or that I can offer something they already haven't considered. But I am recalling a recent video a friend shared with me that was an example of how we can respond, in small ways that will impact the larger picture, possibly in ways we never thought were possible.

In the video a young boy had decided he would make some sandwiches to give to homeless children, but his family was very close to losing their home and barely had enough money to feed themselves. So he set out on foot to ask people if they would help him. Some people frowned at him and walked hastily away, some people listened but did not want to risk having their contributions possibly sold for money, and some took the boy shipping for things he would need. Pretty soon the whole neighborhood in which he lived was involved in the project, even to the point of helping deliver them to people.

Then one day a city official came to his home and asked if he had a permit to do this act of kindness. Of course he didn't so he was asked to not do it anymore. He was confused about this intervention and wondered why an act of kindness had a law around it that would not allow him to continue. His family was sad for him, too. Then his parents came up with an idea. Why not invite families with young children to come to their house and feed them in the back yard? It was their house, their yard, and their act of hospitality. So they proceeded to put the plan in motion.

There is so much more to the story, about how grocery store people helped, how it all created such a crowd that after a while some kind, understanding people stepped in to help and now there is an establishment, approved of by the city and other legal offices, where the young boy, now a teenager, spends much of each day preparing his famous sandwiches which homeless families can stop by to receive. He is 100% in the black financially. His mother helps people mend their clothes, his father helps repair their camping equipment, his younger sister helps in the clothes washing room. And, there is much more to the story.

There was no grand plan—just a desire to help out a few folks with a sandwich. A little thing, but it sparked something that serves the world. The family has to limit how many families they can help per week, along with other limits, but it has changed the face of a neighborhood. Little things like this may not change the whole world, but since we can't be everywhere all the time, what we do in our one small place can make a world of difference. Especially when done with love and caring. We often think the word "world" means the whole globe, but the world can be as small as our neighborhood or home.

RELATIONSHIPS

In 1966 Bob and I, our two children, ages 4 and 5, and Peter the family poodle, boarded a plane and headed for Tokyo, Japan where we lived for the next four years. Bob had a contract to teach high school at the American School in Japan, which is a private school established by business men from around the world for their children. After one year of staying home until Jeff was in school, I signed a contract to teach at the elementary school. The staff for both schools were made up of people from all over the world and our classrooms were filled with children for whom English might have been their second or third language.

Today, April 27, 2015, in my dentist's office a woman asked me what my profession had been. When I told her I had been a teacher, she shared that she and her family had spent 40 years teaching around the world. I mentioned the American School and her eyes teared up as she shared that their most memorable time was the years they spent in Tokyo teaching at the American School in Japan. We hugged in agreement because it was true for Bob and I, as well.

They arrived in Japan in 1970, two months after we left. She taught at the elementary school and had, in her fourth grade classroom, many of the students I had just had in the third grade. We shared the surprises and joys of meeting 40+ years later and agreed on the impact of "building a relationship that lasts a lifetime." In our case, a relationship with an amazing school that is still thriving because of its vision of international oneness, but most of all with its varied staff a staff and a heart-bonding relationship with another culture and its people, who not so long ago were our enemies. Add to this a personal relationship with one's self and one's family that becomes stronger because it has opened to a new way of being in the world where you are the minority, the foreigner.

This year from January to this morning—Tuesday April 28—a new relationship has begun with another "across the years" kind of scenario. The husband of one of Bob's former secretaries made his transition. He had the room just next door to where Bob is in his memory care facility. His wife and I have spent a lot of time sitting with our husbands over the past few months and also talking with each other, sharing our life stories and our faith. We have made a heart connection, that while new, was really begun thirty-plus years ago when she and Bob worked together. Another relationship that proves to me, once again, that whatever relationships we build, at whatever time in earth history, for them to last they must be tended to and nurtured, even in abstentia, because these relationships were sent our way to enrich our lives and to help us grow in and with Spirit.

People come together for all kind of reasons. Some for easily identifiable good reasons, some challenge us and have us asking "why?" Positive relationships improve our life in all aspects, strengthening your mind, your health, your connections to others. In the same vein, it could be one of the greatest drains if the relationship is not working. What is true, if we are willing to look beyond appearances, is that relationships are an investment—the more we add to them from the place of love, caring, commitment, along with a willingness to adapt and change, the stronger and more productive they will be for all. The mind set of those of us at ASIJ helped create lasting relationships that shaped and enriched the rest of our lives. The same is true for Bob and his former secretary and others he worked with who I now get the privilege of interacting with. We set the intention of keeping those relationships alive because we knew they had helped us grow and we wanted to honor them…and, keep the surprises coming, which they certainly have.

IN TUNE WITH
EACH OTHER

Sometimes I go online to either YouTube or Facebook to see if I can find one of my favorite kinds of posts which are those that show such places as a railway terminals, town squares, hotel lobbies and sometimes fronts of restaurants, or other open areas where people walk by on their way to the business of their lives,—though it could be just about any area that crowds of people might be. Into those spaces, unbeknown to others who are going about the business of their lives, people will come and begin playing an instrument and as they do, others come onto the scene doing the same thing until there is a small orchestra playing hauntingly beautiful music, or a group of singers coming together to form a choir-like formation and begin singing, one voice at a time, arias or show tunes, etc.

People passing become intrigued, stop for a moment, shedding their serious expressions and breaking into smiles as their eyes light up in recognition of the magic of the moment. Pretty soon fairly sizable crowds form and stand close together, sometimes taking pictures with photographic devices, or just standing still and letting the music wash over them. On some occasions dancers emerge and express joy through their movements and people watch with amazed focus. I'm sure most of us have resonated with these events.

Whenever these things happen, it is incredible how people are able, in spite of age, ethnicity, life circumstances or musical preference, to stand elbow to elbow and just listen and observe, and be present, seemingly without thought about anything else. At least for a moment or two. To some it is the kind of experience that they have to capture on video or in photos. For others it is just a time to listen, to breathe and to share in the feeling of joy from experiencing the transportation to another reality that touches the soul. At those times everyone is bathed in oneness as a people and in focus.

To me that is the way life is supposed to be. These times need not be the extra ordinary, but the ordinary. Not just in the moment of the shared ecstasy that music can provide, but in each facet of our lives. This is what I believe music keeps trying to teach us. Our souls know this, our souls long for harmony like this, to be bathed in the music of our commonality, not in the disharmony of our perceived or actual differences.

I was five years old, taking piano lessons and singing at church sometimes, when my mother took me to my first film, which was about the lives of famous composers. I remember being awestruck about the beauty of the music, though at that age I couldn't express it well so I just kept it inside, using the remembrance of that music when I had to experience some rough spots as a child, or when I sang to my dolls while playing house. Sometimes I sang church hymns, sometimes I made up songs that I tried to do in a more classical style that I'm sure would have made some of the composers cringe, but I knew I had to have music in my life even beyond the singing I did in church and the piano lessons.

Those experiences at times seemed like a real drag because I was still too young to understand the need for the discipline these things required and I rebelled and wanted to get out of being "forced" to do them. That movie, however, was the turning point for me—or maybe I was growing up a bit—in any case I got it how music had to be a part of my life experiences no matter what it entailed. It was because of the constancy of music that I was able to put aside some impactful personal feelings and learn to love others in my smaller world of school, church and family rather than reject them.

I listened to a recording recently of "the music of the spheres"—actual recordings of the sounds that can be heard when one is out in space. The person recording these sounds described the sounds as perhaps what they were referring to as "angels singing at the time of Jesus' birth." The recordings were soothing, so gentle and so expansively beautiful that I found myself tearful as I listened. The universe singing. The cosmos providing music we are hearing for the first time. What could be more beautiful?

WHAT CAN I SAY,
WHAT CAN I DO

H e stood in the doorway of my office, young, tall, healthy, confused—asking me the questions I'm often asked as a minister when people come seeking guidance, affirmations of hope, but most of all, answers. "I don't know what to do or say about the mess the world is in. It all seems so pointless," he said. "I'm confused. Do I go ahead with my own life, or not? Or do I go out and fight for something, choose one humanitarian cause and make that my focus?"

How deeply I understood the question, especially in light of the world challenges that have presented their claims to us in just the past year: Iraq, the tsunami, bombings, Rwanda, the Terry Schaivo case, and many others, including controversies surrounding recent elections and the coming change in papal leadership with accompanying religious implications.

In response to this questioning young man and to the questions of my own heart, I look to the teachings that have been around for thousands of years to guide and sustain me today. These come from many cultures, faiths, and wisdom teachings, but their truths never change. I want to have them ingrained in my cellular memory and entwined into my DNA, and the soul of every being on the planet: Be generous in prosperity, thankful in adversity. Be loving in speech and fair in interactions. Be a lamp to those who are walking in darkness, a light by example to those who seek the way of Spirit. Be a home to the stranger, eyes to the blind, ears for the deaf, support for those who stumble. Make your life a prayer. Serve where needed. Love your enemy. Do good to those you may perceive hate you. Forgive those who take your goods. Withhold nothing out of spite, anger or selfishness. To those who ask for your cloak, give them a coat as well. Tell others of their goodness. Refrain from judging. Bless those who curse you. Pray for those who abuse you.

Be a breath of life to all, a peacemaker in times of trouble, a teacher of love and respect for all children so they may know their beauty and follow in kind. Hold the hand of those who are dying and help them see the value of their life while on this earth. Walk in humility, yet know your God-given power and use it wisely. Know that God is always there for you, wherever you are. As you wish others would do unto you, do so unto them likewise. Comfort those who mourn. Love and care for your earth home. It's your gift from God.

These truths call me to positive actions, no matter what happens in the future. Practicing these truths, I will have had "something to say and "something to do and give" that will make a difference wherever I journey.

May these ageless ideas help my young friend and contribute to the understanding of the sacredness of all our paths. As you and I act accordingly, peace will be ours.

Participating

⸺⊹⸺

"We don't have to engage in grand, heroic actions to participate in the process of change. Small acts, when multiplied by millions of people, can transform the world."

—Howard Zinn

THE CHURCH OF TODAY: HAPPINESS IN A TIME WARP

A message from Rev. Sherry Lady

My sister's birthday happens this week. We are seven years apart in age and, outside of sharing a bedroom and a closet in our growing up years, and chores related to farming in rural Oregon, we never attended school in the same building, never rode the same school bus, did not share the same personal friends, and weren't able to share clothes due to very different body structures. Even today she is much shorter than I am, has much smaller feet, a rounder face and streaks of very blonde hair still visible among the gray-white patches. I became a teacher; she became a nurse practitioner majoring in pediatrics. I taught in many different schools in several locations; she spent her career at one pediatric clinic in the same town. Yet in spite of so many differences, including living in different places, we share so much internally. Due to the family in which we grew up, the shared values, and the caring we felt for each other through the years, we have remained very close.

Tonight, in celebration of her birthday, we spent almost an hour on the phone together. We talked about our parents, the past we shared, the thoughts and feelings we have about various aspects of life, and the utter confusion we feel at times during this time in history. Like many people, we asked ourselves how this world—and, particularly the country we love so much—got turned upside down so fast as to leave us breathless, often quite confused, and sometimes depressed in spite of our spiritual faith. On top of these strangely spinning changes came the virus, which added to the confusion and radically altered how we do life each and every day. Knowing that each age or generation faces its own challenges, both of us still expressed a longing for days gone by—a simpler, gentler, more hopeful way of life, and a return to the excitement that was abundant after the close of World War II. We both remember that time and the sense of moving forward with positive outlooks. We had a kind of happiness that we wanted each and every one on earth to experience.

After the call with my sister ended, I came across this quote from Pope Francis which is so powerful in its simplicity and its wisdom. I emailed it to my sister and she agreed that it put a lot of things in perspective, including how we can learn from all of Divine creation. Maybe you will enjoy it, too.

> *Rivers do not drink their own water, trees do not eat their own fruit, the sun does not shine on itself, flowers do not spread their fragrance for themselves. Living for others is a rule of nature. We are all born to help each other. No matter how difficult it is…Life is good when you are happy; but much better when others are happy because of you."*

How beautiful life is when we can be a conduit that brings forth happiness from within others. It reminds me the song, which I shared a few weeks ago titled "Make Someone Happy," written by one of our congregants, Alan Reeder. It includes these lyrics:

*The road of life is a lonesome road, if you
must walk it alone.
Reach out and grab a lonesome hand, and
hold it as long as you can.
There's so many people who live all alone,
and wait for someone to see them.
You can be the gift, the savior of one, by
simply reachin' to meet one.
You don't have to be an expert on life,
Or have a degree to listen.
Take time to give time to someone
In need, and see if these words aren't
Worth heed'n.
If you can make someone happy—Do it now.
If you are happy—show them how…*

So I ask myself: What now? Well, tomorrow I go to see my rheumatologist. I am wondering if there will be a moment during that visit to bring forth a smile from someone. Will I remember to smile at people who pass by me? I have to take an elevator to the 8th floor and, in these times, it will be a solo journey. Will I remember to be thankful that I don't have climb eight flight of stairs, especially dragging my walker with me (even though I've done it for three flights once before)? My lawn care people will be here—because of the overwhelming noise of the equipment I often avoid them. Will I remember to smile and be grateful? I'm having guests for dinner on my deck. Will I open and be fully present to them and offer my best? Will I be fully open to receive their loving presence, which they always bring, so they will know how happy they make me feel when we are together? I pray that I will because these days are so full of questions, uncertainties, and lack opportunities to connect in the ways we once did, which we all need so much. Perhaps more of us might consider adjusting how we are present with each other to bless people as much as possible.

In her poem, "Artistic Freedom," Elena Mikhalkova wrote:

> *Don't think about the future, or what may happen tomorrow…Wash the dishes…Remove the dust… Write a letter…Make a soup…Take a step…Rest a little…Then another…And the time will come when you can think about the future without crying.*

You All make me Happy—and I thank you for that.

Love,

Sherry

HOPE, PATIENCE
AND BALANCE

Three items of interest came across my desk this week and when I sat down to write to you, I could not decide which one to share, so I am sharing all three, in the hopes that each item will have some meaning for the reader at this time of transition in our world, and particularly in our country since this is where we have the opportunity, in this moment, to reshape and create what will become our future from this moment on. Perhaps you have seen these before, and if you have, perhaps something new and relevant will come into your awareness, as it did in mine.

First: Caterpillars and HOPE

Caterpillars are so interesting in that they are filled with transformational things called "imaginal cells" and most spectacularly transform from little bits of bug-like life into something of larger and completely different form and shape. The imaginal cells within them are the ones to help them to transform into the beautiful and harmonious butterfly. Each of us express certain qualities of imaginal cells. We are awakening to a new possibility. Using our power to create change, we are clustering—somewhat virtually right now—into a more coherent signal of Love. Be encouraged as our world, which is itself an imaginal cell, begins shape shifting into a more harmonious expression. Help us envision and embody behaviors and beliefs that will nurture a brighter, more beautiful future. Do this by staying HOPEFUL!

Secondly: The Buddha and PATIENCE

To paraphrase one of the teachings of the Master Buddha: When the upper becomes the lower, and the lower becomes the upper; and the inner becomes the outer and the outer becomes the inner. When the male becomes the female and the female becomes the male, then shall we together, not separately, but as one, then shall we enter the Kingdom of enlightenment. This takes courage, insight, fortitude, faith, determination, and the ability to achieve integration in our lives—and it takes a great deal of PATIENCE because such integration does not come easily in a competitive world. Yet, It is the path to wholeness and peace for all. Be patient. We can and will make it if we keep the faith, commit to the practice, and help each other along the way.

Thirdly: Anthropology and BALANCE

A friend sent me an article from our local newspaper written by Doyle Rice. Rice explains that the mass of all our planets human-produced materials exceeds the mass of all life on Earth and its biomass. In fact, the average amount of materials created by humanity every week outweighs the human population! Perhaps one we face reality and truly grasp these shocking figures, we will begin to take responsibility for getting things back in BALANCE.

Anthropologist Margaret Mead was asked by a student what she considered to be signs of civilization in a culture. Her answer was unexpected, She said that the first sign of civilization in ancient cultures was a thighbone that had been broken and then healed. She then explained that with a broken thigh bone you cannot run from danger. If pursued, no one, human or otherwise, survives long enough for the bone to heal.

A broken femur that has healed is a sign that someone has taken time to stay with the one who fell, has bound up the wound and either cared for the one with the broken bone where they are, or carried them to safety and aided in their recovery. Mead said, "We are at our best when we serve others. That is being civilized."

Reinforcing Mead's thought is this note I just received from my daughter: "If you break a bone, calcium forms at the break sight. The calcium is very strong. Stronger than the bone itself which actually weakens during the healing process. During the healing process the membrane around your bone turns into bone and fills the gap where the break was. Eventually the bone heals back to its original strength. We, too, can be calcium for others. We can be strong while others are weak and need time to heal."

As we enter into a new era of history, that will gradually transform our fractured politics of today, may we with HOPE and PATIENCE remember the unstoppability of Divine Grace. May this inspire us to continue seeking BALANCE even amidst times that seem unsteady. With BALANCE we can move toward uncovering, acknowledging and practicing the support of our universal family. We can begin to unify with Divine calcium of spiritual Love, compassionate outreach and caring. As these qualities merge with unconditional acceptance and universal forgiveness, we will form an ever-stronger union not only within our own country, but also around the world, in ways we have never known before.

As we enter into a new era of history may we allow unstoppable Divine Grace to inspire us to merge with unconditional acceptance and universal forgiveness, forming an ever stronger union within our country and around the world in ways we have never known before. God has blessed America. May America bless the world.

Love,

Sherry

THE DIVINE DANCE

Sitting across the table from a good friend at dinner one evening discussing all sorts of various and sundry things about life, we were occasionally distracted, and happily so, by bursts of laughter from a group of eight men seated at a table close by. They seemed to have been friends for a long time and their conversations appeared to have mutual meaning for all of them.

The clink of beer glass toasts punctuated both conversation and laughter, confirming the joy they felt in being together. We later learned they had all been members of the same softball team and were enjoying sharing stories and memories.

"Open minds, open hearts," my friend said, referring to the eight men. When I asked about that statement, I was given the opportunity to find deeper meaning in the interactions we witnessed between the eight men at that table. "Just observe," was suggested. And so, I did. I noticed that as they shared stories together, there was evidence of hearts that were wide open, coming from minds that did not see differences in ages, physical builds, intelligences, mannerisms, or any other thing that might have put a damper on their shared experience. Nothing else mattered but their being together at that moment in time, and joy was fully present.

I realized I was witnessing an important moment that, if carried forth into their daily lives, would be a perfect model for us to see: how when we focus on the good in life, the expectations, judgements, and evaluations we've released become unimportant and we feel our connection to each other in meaningful ways. Deep down inside I believe we all long for this way of living—living in unconditional acceptance of who we and all our "buddies" are so we can lighten the everyday load and allow Divine Peace, Love and Wholeness to flow through us.

When we can open our minds to this unconditional way of thinking, our hearts naturally open as well and our whole being is filled with a Divine presence that brings more joy than we ever thought possible. When each thought that comes to us is unfettered and full of the all-encompassing acceptance of not only what is, but of what is possible, we change everything about our lives, including health, environment, the future, and our relationships to all aspect of life including the transformational acceptance of who is walking with us on this planet at this time, in this life, regardless of size, shape, age, gender, or color, among other things. That seemed to be the environment at the table with the softball friends, and I felt a deep respect and caring for them.

I remember when I was a young girl, one of the assistants in the classroom of my large elementary school took my hands and danced around in circles with me when I was despondent over the death of my best friend. She danced with me until the tears stopped and I felt light of heart again. Her skin was of a different color and this fact could have kept her from reaching out to me. However, I knew her to be one of the most loving and accepting persons in my life at that time. She used to say to us in the classroom:

"Don't shut down that thinking thing in your head or close up that thumping heart." She would sometimes have us put our hands on our heads and over our hearts. I had forgotten about her through the years, but the words of my friend on this evening brought it all back, and I'm so grateful.

The Dalai Lama said, in quoting from the Buddha: "If you can see yourself in others, then whom can you harm?" The Divine dance in which we are invited to participate each day of our lives is one that, as we swing and sway with the daily ups and downs, invites us to take hold of each other's hands and come up higher in consciousness so we can open our minds to what can be. As we do so our hearts open also, and the love therein can come pouring out to be spread about and bring light to the far corners of a place I call "the everywhere."

GROWING WHERE YOU
ARE PLANTED

s I pulled into the parking space at the grocery store,
I received an out-of-character email from a friend
who lives in another state that left me pondering what
was going on, as there was no explanation—just a quote
and a couple of XXOOs at the end. It read: "There are no
boundaries in the universe. Boundaries are illusions—the
way we map reality, and while it is fine to map out the
territory, it is fatal to confuse the two." I immediately
wondered what I had said or done that this needed to be
pointed out to me. As I soon found out, it was perhaps,
"in woo-woo" philosophy, a kind of heads-up message
from the universe.

When I had finished shopping and was pushing my cart
up to the check stand, a young boy who was not looking
where he was heading, ran headlong into the back of my
legs. He was followed by another little boy chasing him and
a frustrated mother trying to catch up with them. In the
"community garden" of the grocery store, both the mother
and I assumed we could do our work within our individual
boundaries, but the young ones were aware of neither. They
were, like meandering cucumber or squash vines, fully into
the joy of unstructured activity.

In that moment I was aware that I had a choice. I could have gotten very angry and let both the children and mother know that they had crossed a boundary with me, this was my territory and I was not happy, which momentarily I wasn't. But when the young boy turned and looked at me with wide eyes filled with fear, I could not help but begin to laugh, smile and tell him it was ok—along with reminding him he needs to be more careful next time about running around in a store. His mother was very apologetic as well as fearful. She also had tears in her eyes, which was the crowning heart-melt moment. She just said "It's so hard with these kids. They have so much energy and are all over the place." I replied, "Yes. I get it. I am all over the place too in my mind, just don't have the energy anymore to do much about it." Then she laughed and gave me a hug—yep, right there in the grocery store.

I don't share this to show or brag about my better side—I do have the flip side as well. Some of you know that and have experienced it. Consider the quote with which I began, about the fatal nature of confusing territories and boundaries. The issue is how we respond. Like that saying, "For every 60 seconds of anger, you lose one whole minute of happiness." Whether it be on the human level or on a cosmic level of understanding, we are the embodiment of a greater consciousness that lives forever and is eternal. There is a power within that can uplift any circumstance in our lives, because our pure nature is love.

Acceptance, compassion, and love are the nutrients of the human garden that allow us to thrive, grow, and eventually expand the territory of our lives beyond what we thought possible.

A favorite quote of mine I'd like to share:

We are Heaven sent to realize Heaven on Earth. In actuality, Heaven is Earth for earth is heaven's physical manifestation. Reality is where Heaven makes landfall. This is it. For Heaven is Love, for Love is Heaven. This is earth and all its inhabitants, Love. Pure love—sent from above. We, humankind and all of nature's kind are 'that'…The Garden of Eden is right here on earth. Don't look for it anywhere else. We truly have arrived. We have manifested. We only need to realize it. Let us realize that the world is the more beautiful of realities.

Yes, we are the embodiment of the cosmic consciousness Jon talked about last Sunday. So smile, laugh, love—and yes, grieve, and grow, and change, and glow. These are the rainbow colors of your eternal cosmic soul. They are all part of that embodiment and will bring you back home to love.

As to those energetic boys, I bought each a pineapple popsicle and shared my thoughts about what a grocery store was intended to be used for. I mentioned that if this happened again and I was caught unprepared again, they would have to buy me a popsicle. They thought that was funny. "What if we never see you again?" one boy asked. "That would be my loss," I replied "because I'd like to buy you another popsicle sometime." Who knows? At least the seed got planted.

A SURPRISING SONG

"Take courage, for the human race is Divine," wrote Pythagoras, the great Greek philosopher of the sixth century, B.C.

As I read over this statement I admit to feeling a little discouraged by the date of this statement. If what he says is true, why have we taken so long to accept, internalize and act upon this aspect of our being? Why do we still have wars, cruelty, injustice, greed, anger, hate, etc. and why do we experience tragic things that take us out of feeling our divinity and plunge us deep into fear and uncertainty—like what we are experiencing around the world at this time? Divinity has always had, for me, the quality of a kind of closeness to our creator that makes it possible to be peaceful no matter what.

This afternoon while watering plants out on my deck, I checked in with my geraniums. They didn't say much, but they continued to present their collective best unencumbered by anything other than the will to continue to grow in the afternoon sun. As I looked at how the clusters of small petals made up the whole I decided that the answer might be that even though there are collective aspects to our journey, the basic human journey toward realization of this divinity is made individually, one by one. However, at times we may lean a bit on the arms of another, like the blossoms lean on the stalk—and on me—for the water.

Edgar Cayce suggests that we journey home best when we take the arm of someone else and let them lean on us. When we do this, we step out of ourselves and the pure energy of Divine can flow through a body system that is fully open to love, caring and kinship. From this we grow and move on to eventually learn how to be more fully our divine selves. This seems so obvious in this present moment when, even though we can't see, touch or hug each other in the way that we like to do, people are reaching out through whatever means possible and in ways they might not have done before, to assure others that they are loved and cared for and important. I see, feel and experience this in ways that assure me daily that I am not alone, and as a result I can truly say, "my cup runneth over."

From the geraniums I moved to where the lilies have pushed up and out of their winter resting place to stand strong and tall in their white glory. Perhaps they are saying "I am here. I hope you can see how I have come out from the dark night of winter soil to remind you to stand tall along with me for the world needs reminding of the presence of pure hope and strength" We are being called upon to stand taller than ever these days, not in a proud stance of the conquering hero, but as one who overcomes—one who pushes up through the places where we are in resistance to what is so as to affirm our divinity. Not a divinity of arrogance, but of affirmation that we know the truth of the source of our being and with that we can overcome that which needs to be overcome. And—to hold out Hope for the world.

Hope was hard to come by when while watching TV I saw large tractors moving through 500 acres of green beans and plowing them under because there was no market for them and they were prevented from giving them away then

200 acres of ripening tomatoes also being given back to the earth by green Caterpillar tractors, while at the same time the reporter was telling us that food pantries cannot keep up with the needs of the unemployed and are running out of food for the homeless, and all the families that are facing hunger. I wondered what the lilies would say about this if they could talk.

Along with many of you, I am attempting to stand tall in the midst of that chaos, because I know there are thousands of people out there attending to the details of the chaos, sacrificing everything as they stand tall in their calling. They are truly the Lilies of the field—inviting the crowds of geranium petals to join them in whatever way possible. So I am choosing to see the divinity in all of them, in all my friends who are reaching out to lend an arm, in all the people everywhere who are expressing their divinity through prayer, holding the high watch through sending out vibrations of love and gratitude, and connecting with others through various means while also doing their part by staying home staying safe at home and holding out Hope for the days ahead.

We can do this. We can be strong. We can still find things to smile about and people to laugh with. We can sing and dance in hallways and showers, and do what needs to be done because as our individual courage is called forth to shine, we learn to know the truth of who we are: beings quite capable of showing our connection to The One.

There are many songs yet to be sung. And many more Springs yet to come.

THE BEST TIME

Sunday night I found myself watching a PBS evening presentation on the history and stories of the various wars, the leaders at the time and the sequence of events. I know, what was I doing watching that kind of thing? I was watching for two reasons: it had come up in a group conversation at a gathering earlier in the day and then a friend suggested that watching it might give us even more insights into the world as we know it today. It did in many ways and I'm glad I watched it—all 3 hours of it.

What came to mind this morning, as a result of taking the time to watch the presentation, were three questions asked in a children's story and three similar points discussed in a recent lecture by a spiritual teacher with whom I have become reacquainted. They left me with much to think about. The three are:

1. When is the best time to do things?

2. Who is the most important right now?

3. What is the right thing to do?

Things to hold in mind about the "best time":
We often think "now" as in "now or never." However, I

feel that sometimes it is best to watch, pay close attention, get more information, and ask who will this affect and how before stepping into action. However, when a decision is needed in the interest of others' health, safety, or wellbeing, then by all means "now is the time." That also holds true for decisions about one's own life, future, fulfillment of dreams, etc. In those cases, there is no time like the present and "now is the time." Would that this has been the response to recent scientific information that was pushed aside. As we are finding out these days, many times it is more difficult to cure a deep wound than to avoid causing it in the first place.

Regarding the "most important person":

We can do some of life by ourselves but most of the time we need others to be a part of this journey. We need others to help with decisions, give support, share love and compassion, jeep us from feeling lonely or fearful, and hold the high watch when we are not feeling strong. Leaning on each other is not a weakness but an affirmation of our belief in each other. The most important person for us is the one we are with, whenever we are. Sometimes we have several at a time. That is when our "cup runneth over."

About "the right thing to do":

One of the greatest teachings found in all religions is paraphrased in these familiar words: "Do unto others as you would have them do unto you." The "right thing to do" is always to do "good" for the one by your side. This is why we are here. Romans 12:17—"Repay no evil for evil, but do what is honorable and food in the sight of all." Who is standing by our side? Who is there for us to share good with and to love? To Love—with a capital L—is the right thing to do, as is taking care of others and being there in times of need. Like stones cast into water, the ripples of the deed reach further than we can see, beyond our imagination.

Now I'll add a fourth question: "How do we respond to the future?" Once the challenge we face is over, the life we knew as normal is never coming back. It may feel like doom and gloom, but it is a reality we all will be facing. This is our opportunity to carry with us all the things that come to matter more and more, all that we treasure, that we can use to enhance our days and lives, and to finally create that world we have longed for deep in our souls. It will not be easy. We will all have some time-warp PTSD to deal with and confusion to clear up as a result of a virus altered life. But we do have our spiritual "tools" that have not disappeared and have been with us through it all, to help us establish more visibly the "kingdom of heaven on earth." And, if we are willing, we have each other to support us on our journey.

THE BUSINESS OF
THE UNIVERSE

W ell known author Byron Katie has shared this obser-
vation: *I find only three kinds of business in the universe: mine, yours and God's. Much of our stress comes from
mentally living out of our own business.*

Just imagine how much different your life would be
if you were somehow able to stay focused solely on your
own business? Imagine the freedom. You wouldn't have
to worry about what your spouse was doing, because that
would be their business. You wouldn't get upset about what
your neighbor is doing or not doing because that is their
business, and you wouldn't waste energy complaining about
the weather, because that's God's business. You would be
free to focus on yourself.

Now that may seem very self-centered, uncaring, and
almost flippant if stated in uninformed ways. But let's take
a look at that. When you are free to focus on yourself—and
you have allowed your inner Christ-guide-intuition-inner
knowing, however you want to label it, to develop, you have
created the perfect space for you to move in the direction of
your heart's calling. It also leaves you free to take action on
those things that you have so wanted to do in your daily life,
and most beautiful of all, it allows you to be there to care for

others as well. By focusing on yourself and paying attention to what is yours to do that day or that moment and acting upon it, you will begin to see how Spirit works to guide you to the areas where you will not only be a blessing to others, but will reap abundant joy for yourself. I believe if we all practiced focusing on our own business and asked, from that space of freedom within ourselves, what is mine to do today—only mine—and then acted upon that in the sphere of our unencumbered freedom space, a huge shift would happen in our lives and in the world. We would actually be able to, no matter the chaos that is swirling, "Love what is."

EGGSACTLY LIKE US

S ix kids, including me, varying in ages from 5-8, sat around a table that had a large bowl of color dyed, hard boiled Easter eggs in the center. We had finished our hunt out in the yard and emptied our baskets into the bowl. The object was to practice sharing by dividing the total between us so that everyone had the same amount of eggs. Then we could each unpeel one and, with a little salt, have a snack, before diving into the candies that were also collected.

What happened, I remember clearly, was that while the adults went to sit and share a cup of coffee, us kids found that peeling the eggs, taking out the yolks and putting them back into the bowl so we could eat just the whites, was so much fun that we did that all of the eggs. That left a bowl of yolks as a centerpiece and lots of egg shells scattered around the table. I've laughed about that memory through the years, but have forgotten the outcome as far as what the adults did with our ingenuity.

Through the years, eggs became a representation of the empty tomb from which Jesus emerged, as well as signs of fertility and rebirth into new life. They were not allowed to be eaten during Holy Week, but were saved for the children and given to them on Easter. Victorians decorated cardboard eggs and gave them as gifts. In the 19th century the bunny became the deliverer because they were prolific at bringing new life into existence. In Switzerland the eggs were delivered by the cuckoo bird and in Germany by the fox.

So why am I telling you all this? Let's look at it this way: (bear with me here) Egg whites contain needed protein, while the yolks contain vitamins A, D, E and K, along with omega-3 fats and are rich in folate and vitamin B-12. They are also packed with tryptophan, tyrosine and amino acids that help prevent heart disease. In essence, it is a perfect food, and both parts are needed to do that. I'm not suggesting everyone eat eggs, but what I am suggesting is there is a possible universal and spiritual teaching in just considering the symbolism of the item that has become so much associated with the holiday we celebrate this time of year in our tradition.

The outer serves a basic and necessary purpose. The inner is richer and more extensive in what it provides, though it is best partnered with the outer as well. So are we. On the outer we are encased in a beautiful and strong body full of life, energy, dreams, activities, etc. that holds us together and lets us move about in our life, but it is the inner that will provide us with the nourishment, sustenance, and stability to be all that we can be while here in this life.

The message of this symbol then becomes about importance of the whole to give fertility to the role we have assumed here on earth and will help us be reborn anew each and every day through the gift we have been given of life here and now. Like the Spirit of the Christ we can emerge into our fullness and, with Spirit, resurrect ourselves to the elevation for which we were intended. An egg has a shell to protect it until it is ready to be and serve on its own—much like a parent or family, and sometimes as a hard-protective shell we won't let go of in order to move on. At Easter time, and any time we are willing, we have an awesome opportunity to break through the shell of resistance and become the best "eggs" we can.

This is ever more poignant at the confusing and interruptive and crazy time in our lives and the world. Let's hold for ourselves and for each other that in spite of what appears to be a crazy in the protective shell of our lives, what's inside is "hard boiled" enough to remain strong and to emerge from this place into a world, ready to courageously and with renewed vigor and commitment, begin again to be a bravely confident, better informed, creative and more compassionate and loving world both at home and everywhere Spirit leads us.

FEELING FREE TO BE ME

Sent to me by my daughter Julie, on a day when things were not going well and she decided to take some refuge in her newly purchased book "The 7 Story Mountain" by Thomas Merton.

Thoughts on a quote from Thomas Merton: "It takes a heroic humility to be yourself and be nobody but the [person], or artist, that God intended you to be."

I'm thinking about Krissy, who with the other counselors worked with teens—teens that just sit in a room unwilling to talk. I think about the two years I lived in my big house in a "room," a sort of office, with my arms crossed, refusing to let God speak because it seemed I wasn't being spoken to anyway. I think about my friend, who after the loss of a child, said she is "ignoring HIM." I understand. We can ignore God until we hit a wall with our doing and then God says "BE." How can we do this though, when our doing is what we think will make things all right? How can I "BE" when I live in a society that proudly wears the Nike swoosh of "Just Do It"? How can I just "BE" when my doing is how I've thought I best serve others? Formulas for success: 12 steps, Seven Habits of Highly Successful People, perfect hair, perfect anything in 3 easy steps, checklists, grocery lists, progress monitoring, and on and on.

Then comes the terrifying reality—the universe doesn't really support any of this and God doesn't really seem to care. Spirit is probably glad when we're nice to people—if that's how it works—but only if it's sincere because most people know when we aren't.

We are supposed to take care of the planet, be wise about spending our money, etc. but only if we have a sincere desire to do so. If not, no one is really impressed, least of all God. And even with the biggest love, best of intentions, pure hearts, etc. it can fall apart. It can ALL fall apart, and we never know why.

Then there is also humility. Yes, humility is heroic because it takes hero-sized courage to admit that we are incapable of pleasing God by being anything other than ourselves. We are afraid of what will happen if we aren't what we think we should be. I have read quotes by both Mother Teresa and Oprah where they wonder if they are doing what God intended them to do. WHAT?? REALLY?? They must have had the courage and humility to confess that there was still a part of themselves in all their "doing" that was still not quite fully in touch with their being. Nice to know they were/are human like me. They maybe hadn't yet started to "BE."

I've unfolded my arms, and I've decided I'm ready for a conversation with the universe and to listen to what is mine to hear. I'm asking to be shown who I am—and who I was intended to be. The feeling inside is one of incredible freedom! To become fully ME? Is it possible? I want that more than anything. Don't you?

BISCUITS FOR THE SOUL

This week a minister friend of mine sent me this amusing clip, which I will share in just a moment. As a minister of a church in another state, he and his congregation were faced with having to possibly close the church because the small and dwindling rural community was facing financial challenges that made it very difficult to be able to continue to pay him his salary.

He reminisced about how excited he and his wife were when they were called to this then thriving area some 12 years ago. On the first night in their small, supposedly temporary house, they had celebrated their good fortune with a glass of wine, a sumptuous dinner and toasted each other by affirming that they were on the adventure of their lives. Step by step they were going to participate in the building of a thriving congregation that would assure them some financial stability. They were going to rise to the occasion with courage, fortitude and a strength built on faith.

Now, they were faced with unexpected change, their spirits were dampened and they wondered why and how this could happen to them. Weren't they doing what Spirit had guided them to do? Didn't they respond with the knowing that all was in Divine Order? Didn't they pour their hearts and souls into their work? Didn't they follow guidance and pray and meditate daily and espouse to their congregation the benefits of positive thinking? What else could they have done to help create a solid church, while watching the fertile soil produce abundant crops for their farmer congregants and bless them all?

We had several conversations about all that was going on, and then this week, as I mentioned above, I received this little story from them.

"A visiting minister was attending a men's breakfast in Ohio farm country. He asked one of the impressive older farmers in attendance to say a blessing over the meal that morning. When all were seated, the older farmer began—

'Be it known that I hate buttermilk.' (The minister opened one eye and wondered to himself where this was going).

'Be it known that I hate lard.' (Now the visiting minister was really worried). However, without missing a beat , the farmer prayed on. "And be it known I don't care much for raw white flour!'

Just as the minister was ready to stand and stop everything, the farmer continued:

'But be it known that when you mix them all together and bake 'em up, they make fresh, warm, tummy lovin' biscuits. Now when we just don't understand Spirit's ways, or what we're supposed to be doin, we need to just relax and wait 'till Spirit is done mixin', and it will probably come out somethin' even better than biscuits."

The story that he shared with me made me realize how that being there in that small town, with that sweet church was just the beginning, the first step in our ministerial life adventure. It was the place where we were to hone our skills, get clear about the message we wanted to share, learn something more about trusting Spirit, affirm our divine strength and courage and get ready to move on to the next time and place for the next adventure. We like to think that when we thought we had failed, we had actually succeeded in completing a step on the journey. Now, before we leave, we will be able to help our friends make the adjustment for a new way of living and being in their lives.

When we see more clearly, when we allow ourselves to find the place of the heroic spirit within us, when we learn to live with the faith, the knowing that all existences is divine unfolding, we find ourselves living "on friendly terms with a friendly universe, and a very wise Spirit that is guiding us.

Each of us is being called daily to rise up and express our divine strength and courage, to affirm the heroic Spirit within, and to be ready to be changed at depth as we continue our adventure in living.

Thinking now about stirring up a batch of buttermilk biscuits. My favorite strawberry jam is already in the fridge, but will have to go to the store for the buttermilk. Forget the lard. Lord knows I don't like lard either, so I give thanks for alternatives. But most of all I give thanks for my friend, for the little funny stories that show up along the way in life, and that there is a heroic spirit in you and me that helps us recognize the courage and strength we have to be heroes/heroines in our own right without having to wield power over anyone else—just take their hand and walk together. It's in every one of us.

WHEN IT'S TIME TO CLEAN OUT OUR STORAGE

⸺✻✻✻⸺

I opened the taped lid of a somewhat crunched cardboard box, one of many I had retrieved from a storage unit. My good friend Sue stood waiting to assist. It was my daughter's Japanese handwriting practice book which she did while in an elementary classroom at ASIJ (American School in Japan in the second grade. Underneath was my son's book which he had done in the first grade. Memories flooded back, and I had to swallow hard to keep from coming completely undone. "Not this box," I said to Sue. "Not this one, I'm not ready yet." And after several Kleenex and dripping mascara, I set it aside.

So it went over several months. Box after box from my baby shoes to my children's baby shoes to my husband's letterman jacket, the license plate from our first car, a prom dress, and dozens of photo albums and memorabilia. Evenings of sorting with laughing and crying—feelings surfacing and ebbing. Memories of a life well lived, a family well bonded, and knowing I have so much to be grateful for. Many daytime hours were spent cleaning out those boxes, with Sue standing with me through much of it.

Now the task is nearly accomplished, though there are items still scattered all over my house yet to be determined as to the length of their stay here with me. Everything has been examined to the best of my ability and emotional stability at this point. The result is a lightness of being. Wafts of air move through the spaces now cleared, healing light shining through what were once dark, closed-off corners. How good it feels to know that life, even with its ups and downs is still such a precious thing. How freeing to know there is now room for the new, whatever that may be.

DANCING FROM THE
DARK INTO THE LIGHT

His hands were gripping a silver walker and his knuckles made sharp ridges across the tops of his fingers. His back was curbed and his feet were covered with slippers that seemed a bit too large for walking with ease. Moving slowly and deliberately he made his way across the room to the dining area, talking quite loudly as he progressed. HIs eyes were surprisingly bright and his words clear and articulate though they were words of anger and frustration and were spoken with the intention of making them heard by anyone within earshot, though not spoken to anyone in particular. "Goddamn it, none of you know what it's all about. You just think you do. You think you have all the answers. You don't know a damn thing."

Exhausted with the effort of both moving about and speaking with emphasis, he found a recliner in the corner of the dining room and slumped into it. His words became a series of mumblings. His eyes opened wider and anger seemed to shoot out of them. At that point, the visiting musicians who had come to entertain the residents began to play their first song and he slumped back further into the chair and muttered something about being time for his pain pill.

When the second song began, one of the caregivers with a glass of water and a pill cup went over to him, gave him his pill and instead of moving away when he finished, she stood by the chair, said something to him and offered him her hand. His face softened. As she squatted down and continued talking to him, he reached out and took her hand. Then, much to my amazement, she took both of his hands and began to sway to this music. He began to stand up and soon, without the aid of his walker, he took a few steps to one side and then to the other. By then they were both smiling. They swayed to the music and did a bit of foot movement for a few minutes before she helped him back into his chair.

I was able to get her attention and she came over to me. "Tell me what just happened here," I asked. She told me that this man had been a dance instructor at a college back east and it was his life—until he became ill and his daughter moved him here to be close to her. He was very angry at having to move and even angrier that he was not going to get well. He was also 94 but he told everyone he was 56 and was going to get back to work soon. He was difficult to work with except for those times when the caregiver was able to get him up to dance with her. After that he would calm down and be cooperative for an extended period of time. She tried to make sure he danced at least 5 times a week when she was there.

But that's only part of the story, because this caregiver then told me she had lost her husband and son in a car accident 5 years before and had it not been for this aged dance instructor she would have given up on life. He had somehow taken a special liking to her and called her his "beautiful dance partner." She learned from him, when his mind was a bit more clear, that movement releases something very healing from inside one's own being—a spiritual "something" that has the power to carry one through times of trouble. She said she dances at home every time oppression and depression set in. A vital spiritual key in life is learning how to tap into that which is available to carry and guide us through times of trouble. For her, "free dancing" as she called it, did that for her.

Each of us has our own "dance" that can help us through the tough times. Each "dance" will be different—i.e. walking, meditation, prayer, singing, writing, or a combination of those and other tools. But each comes from an innate wholeness that recognizes, through our participation, that we can move from the dark into the Light when we bring forth what is the truth of us.

"Healing may not be so much about getting better, as about letting go of everything that isn't you—all of the expectations, all of the beliefs—and becoming who you are."

—Rachel Naomi Remen

IN THE PRESENCE

⸺⸺⸺

The sun has set over the cottage, but the glow of the still-lighted horizon casts an aura of peaceful warmth, inviting walkers to step onto the garden path and stroll slowly so as to savor the beauty of the evening. Autumn leaves float soundlessly onto the shadows cast by small birch trees, and plants still full of blooms as if it were July instead of October. A gong sounds in the east end of the garden, followed by wind chimes and the sound of a waterfall. An opportunity to put aside cares of the day and step into the now moment.

Stepping into the now moment may be a bit of a stretch for some of the strolling guests, but not for the family members whose hands they hold, or who's wheelchairs they push. Silent in the wonder of it all, those being walked and wheeled, have eyes opened wide, as if seeing each beautiful image for the first time and one is heard to say, "Oh, so beautiful" and another "He like being outside." "He" is the pronoun used to refer to himself. It takes the place of "I," because "I" has no meaning anymore as any sense of the egoic has begun to fade into obscurity, not into memory, because memory is not available any more. One is fully in the present, teaching the "pushers" and "hand holders" what it means to be only there.

Such it was recently on a beautiful evening, in a gorgeous garden, at a place where those with fading memories live and are cared for and where family members gather to adjust to a new way of living in the now moment. Where silence is spoken more often than a plethora of words. Where, beyond belief, one can, in the midst of personal sadness, experience a deeply gratifying walk if one is willing to let go and become one with the experience. There is no deeper place of Now than here where there is no time. Only God.

Eckhart Tolle, in his book "The Power of Now" said it well: "How to stop creating time? Realize deeply that the present moment is all you ever have. Make the Now the primary focus of your life." And, he also wrote "Silence is a potent carrier of Presence." To listen to the silence, wherever you are, is an easy and direct way of becoming present."

HAPPY TO BE HERE—A PRAYER FROM THE HEART

I looked into the dark brown eyes of the person leaning over me and exclaimed "I am so happy to be here." The response to me was appropriate for the setting: "For most people this is one of the last places they want to be." But, I meant what I said, especially after the diagnosis had been given while a gentle hand was wiping my forehead—"Type A flu, with pneumonia, fever 104.3, you will be staying with us for a while." Thank you, God, I could actually pray, in my heart, for I was truly glad to be with professionals. I felt no fear. It was obvious God was there in the person of a very honest, caring physician who just happened to have a sense of humor as well and let me make my ridiculous Carol Burnett kind of statements, which I tend to do while in the midst situations that could present challenges, without judgment. My job, however, in this situation was: To help the physician do his job, to be helpful by supporting the staff and other caregivers. And, of course to do as I was told so I could heal.

No fear, just gratitude for a safe hospital bed. To me that was amazing, because I can be quite cowardly when it comes to health issues that require me to give in to their demands and threaten my need to be independent and in control; but, I was in no position other than to let go completely and let someone else take over. In this case a medical professional, and yet, what stayed with me for the next few days was, and still does, more profoundly than ever, is that wherever I am, God is. I do not have to worry. The God presence will direct me. In fact, the reason we are here, now, is to be the carrier of the God presence everywhere and to see the good in every situation and every person, regardless. Even when its uncomfortable or embarrassing, or confusing.

Together, you and me, have one united purpose: to go where we are led and to be truly helpful in this world, as Spirit guides us. We do some things individually, and many things together, some willingly, some with dragging feet, but with faith we do our work. All else we do, sharing our talents and gifts is what keeps us busy and entertained and productive in the process. With these we can also bless the world and make life's journey more enjoyable. But, bottom line is, we are here to serve. Period.

HOW TO SEE THE MOON

The next full moon will occur this week on Thursday, May 7 at 6:45 ET and is known as the full flower moon. Full moon time is always a very important and special occurrence for me. Perhaps it comes from growing up on a farm where there were open spaces to see the brilliance. Or maybe it is because she represents the feminine aspects of being. I only know that I feel very close to her and always leave the curtains in my bedroom open so I can view her if I wake up at night when she arcs across the sky.

In a recent lecture, given by one of the leaders of a healing tradition that originated in Japan, an example of how to view the moon was given as a guide for learning how to align mind and body for healthy living. I was listening to the lecture via our newest technological pathway called zoom because a number of years had elapsed since I attended two years of classes at a Dojo here in Eugene where universal energy teachings were given, as part of instruction in a healing method called Kiatsu, along with basic martial arts. I did not participate in the martial arts part but was very interested in, and appreciative of, the instruction given in that particular healing method. There is much I could share about that experience, but my purpose here is to share some universal truths that, to this day, are very profound and applicable to all people and all of life everywhere.

The beginning example before the lecture was to remind us that if we want to see the moon in all its glory, and we hold up our hand to point to it, we will miss the experience if we continue to focus on the finger that is pointing in that direction. The finger representing us, and the moon, the universe and all of life, is an interesting and poignant example of we can have a limited view of life. With the thought that the 20th century was one of expanding the material world, in which some of the soul of life was lost, it becomes evident that it is time now, in the 21st century, for us to bring back enhancement of mind and body so as to be able to handle the outcomes of what the 20th century expansion has brought to us at this time.

Rules for daily living were presented and, while it is impossible for me to share the richness of the entire lecture, I am sharing 10 rules that emerged. Not my rules, or the teacher's rules, but the rules of the universe for healthy, happy living with a fully functioning and peaceful mind and body in today's environment.

1. There are universal principles and they are part of all religions. Universal energy (Ki) never stops. It is the origin of all things and in order to thrive within it, we must realize practice and take responsibility for supporting the rules/laws to the best of our ability. We do this by:

2. Practicing love for all creation

3. Being grateful—doing our best—grateful to be alive

4. Doing good in secret. Not hiding it, but recognizing that it is not about us. Do good

because it is the right thing to do.

5. Look upon all creation with merciful eyes and gentle body.

6. Be forgiving and large hearted

7. Think deep and judge (discern) well

8. Be calm and determined, and live a life in which mind and body are unified and have as their purpose the caring for, honoring, and reverence for all of creation.

9. Be positive and vigorous. Try to do everything in a positive way.

10. Persevere while remembering that you are strongest when you are helping others.

Not easy these days of challenges, confusion, fear and uncertainty. I find myself stumbling quite often in my quest to manage each day in a positive way. Therefore, the review of these principles was food for my soul. They served to take my eyes off of the "finger pointing to the moon" (me) and helped to turn my head and eyes in the direction of that beautiful lady who will still be there for us to look upon this week as a constant reminder that looking upward is a better way to face and live life.

Join me in gazing at the moon this week. If it is obscured by clouds, which it often is in Oregon, look upward anyway and let yourself be blessed by the knowing that there is a constant and Divine presence of eternal light there for us, to guide us, even in the darkness.

THE NATURE OF THINGS

G rowing up on a farm was a mixed blessing for me at times. Quite often it became a drudgery for a young girl like me who had no brother to do the heavier things and a little sister seven years younger who was under my wing. I was not often enamored with having to hoe the garden, stack the wood, feed my rabbits, spend summers going from one crop harvest to another, and then spending part of the winters indoors, between school and homework, preparing the strawberry plants for spring planting. However, something worthwhile rubbed off on me I'll have to admit.

The best phrase to sum it up seems to be "the nature of things"; the amazing life-cycle of not only plants and animals, but of the days in the sun and sleeping under the stars at night.. Squishing a strawberry between my fingers and wondering how that berry and its parent plant came from the tiny seed I could barely pick up in my fingers. Watching the trees in the orchard at winter's end to try to catch the emergence of the first bud on the apple tree by my bedroom window before anybody else did. How could a potato plant emerge from that chunk of potato my father put into the ground at just the right time so it would not rot, but would produce next fall's baked potatoes? If I stared at a baby rabbit long enough could I actually see it grow into a bigger rabbit? So many things were incredible to me, and are to this day.

Add to that the wondrous, odiferous oak, fir and pine tree forest up on the hill behind our farm where mother, my sister and I would go when it snowed to take photos of the beauty of winter, or sip lemonade in the summer and take a nap after a day in the fields.. As they dropped their seeds on the ground I used to wonder if I could speed up their process of becoming a big tree by asking God to perform a miracle for me right then and there.

And now, I am often reminded that we all were once a seed of a human form developing in the womb of our mothers, full of potential, part of the universal life-cycle of regeneration and earth replenishment, just like the strawberry, the potato, the fir tree, the apple. And like the snow on the fir and pine trees, some of us have white hair to crown the persona that has unfolded in its own unique ways through time… at one with the Divine plan. In spite of reluctance to face the mirror at times, we can smile and take into our hearts the words "well done" for we have become the elders through whom the spirit of life has emerged to bless the world. At least that's my affirmation, even though I still have a long way to go in being what I could be, but I will get there. It's inevitable, because that's the nature of things.

STRENGTH IN
SMALL THINGS

*"Be faithful in small things because
It is in them that your strength lies."*

—Mother Teresa

There I am, an older woman with white hair, struggling to keep my two grocery bags from sliding off the seat of my walker while trying to look still in control of my physicality and my persona, but knowing others are watching me in my attempt, each with their own version of what the outcome will look like. Out of the onlookers, most of who were walking by a bit more briskly than usual perhaps, there comes toward me a young man who offers assistance. I guess him to be about college age and therefore quite capable. My temptation is to say "Oh, no, thanks, I'm just fine," which is my usual knee jerk response. But something about this young man is different, though I don't know in what way. So I accept, gratefully and he even offers to follow me to my car, which I accept.

When we arrive at the car, I open the trunk and he very carefully places the bags inside. I am impressed by the care he takes. As he closes the lid I thank him and then he asks if I would have time to have a cup of coffee with him. I feel my internal clock saying I should be getting on with the next thing I need to do, but another, stronger nudge says "Why not take time for coffee this one time?" And so we go sit in the outside area near the market, he goes in to order coffee, and returns with a cookie as well. I say to him, "Thank you so much. Surely you must have other things to do than sit with an old grandma type after already doing her a big favor." To which he responds: "Not today because classes haven't started yet." So I smile and say "Tell me more." To which he responds:

"I don't want to talk about my classes right now. I want to say something to you, if you don't mind." I didn't, so he proceeded. "I just got here from my home in South Dakota to go to school up in Washington after I visit friends here. I'll be a Freshman in pre-law. While I was coming here I got the message that my grandmother had fallen, broken her hip and died. She was a lot older than you, but I liked her a lot. I can't go back for the funeral. I didn't get to tell her how much I loved her and to thank her for the $50 she gave me for my trip because I wanted to do that when I called her after getting here. So can I say that to her through you? Can we have coffee and let me pretend you are her right now? It may seem like not much, but it means a lot to me. Her name was Lorraine."

Of course you know my answer, though you may think it strange that I did not ask him more questions. I just gave him my card and told him to let me know how things go, as tears began ruining my mascara. He had done one small thing and I was able to give time to him, thank God, but I know we both felt stronger to face our day, in spite of our years-apart-generation-gap lives.

This, I realized, is how we, through some small gesture, can do great things. Mother Teresa also said:

"I can do things you cannot do; you can do things I cannot do. Together we can do great things."—even in an outdoor coffee area, next to a supermarket, on a warm, early fall day.

Never underestimate the power of seizing the moment to be present for Spirit to do its work through you. It is in these moments when we can let go of our need to do or have things turn out perfectly, like even being in perfect control of shopping bags, or think some things just can't be tended to right now because we haven't time, that life's richest blessings are manifest.

By now many of you might be remembering Mother Teresa's famous saying "Not all of us can to great things, but we can do small things with great love." As a spiritual community let's commit to doing the small things that matter for our spiritual home, and the things we can do for each other, with great love. It is our calling.

RIDING THE WINDS
OF CHANGE

What's on your mind today? I've been thinking about the title on page 2 of our monthly bulletin—"Taking the Ride of Our lives"—and remembering what came to my mind a couple of weeks ago when I experienced a trip back in time. A time when the kid that still lives inside of me, prompted me to head toward the merry-go-round at a well-known pizza place where I, silly me, gave in to temptation. Thanks to a very nice gentleman who helped me onto the bench style seat, since I was pretty sure I could not straddle a horse any longer even though I wanted to, I was able to relive, even if for a moment, what it was like to be a child again.

When we began to move around to the tune of a very lively, lovely melody, I found myself tearing up a bit as I recalled the ride I took on a merry-go-round at a park in Portland when I was about 4 or 5 years old. I can visualize the dress I was wearing because I still have it in my cedar chest. I remember how free and light I felt and how, knowing I had my whole life ahead of me, I felt only joy.. Yes, I was thinking those thoughts even at that age. My mother used to tell me I thought too much about everything, and said I was like that even before I could talk. Photos of me at that age often show a furrowed brow, so maybe she was right. I only remember being puzzled about what life was like as I observed it. Like so many of us, I have pondered what it would be like to ride this life again, only with the knowledge I have now to carry me through.

So –here we are, you and I, once again riding the winds of change in our lives. And, just when we thought we knew how to not get "thrown off the horse" so to speak, and to ride with dignity, endurance and some grace, the winds have brought us to a place where something floating through the air and landing on surfaces so we can touch them and carry it on further, is presenting a menacing face that has left us basically clueless as to what to do about it or how to stop it. None of us were expecting this. What do we do now?

If I had the magic answer, I would be so happy to share it. But I don't. All I can do is not become over-the-top frightened, follow the rules of cleanliness, avoid crowds, and then, in quiet time visualize the threat completing its cycle, leaving as little as possible behind in its wake, and sending out to the world—yes in our community and the whole world—as much love and hope and peace and healing as possible. Thrown into the mix is also a bit of "What are you doing, or not doing, God? And why?" because in spite of my faith and belief that all will be well, I have inside of me that little kid who is relying on the parent to fix things and I have to talk to her/him about it. I have a teddy bear named Good God who is a very good listener. Besides knowing all my secrets he is very wise.

Let's continue to take the positive ride of our lives. Let's continue to ride the winds of change with faith. Let us remember who we are, that we are in this together, that we can make a difference with our attitude and our trust in a higher power to sustain us through absolutely everything. And we can let the lovely melody of the life's happy merry-go-round permeate our very being and lift us higher in consciousness each day because we have been perfect from the beginning and nothing can take that away from us.

Integrating

—◦◦◦◦—

"We are each other's harvest. We are each other's business. We are each other's magnitude and bond."

—Gwendolyn Brooks

A BED BY THE WINDOW

S tarting off with a bit of humor because it is such a good metaphor for life right now:

"During a visit to my doctor, I asked him, 'How do you determine whether or not an older person should be put in an old age home?'

He replied, 'We fill up a bathtub, then we offer a teaspoon, a teacup and a bucket to the person and ask them to empty the bathtub.'

'Oh, I understand.' I said. 'A normal person would use the bucket because it is bigger than the spoon or teacup.'

'No,' he said. 'A normal person would pull the plug. Do you want a bed near the window?'"

We seem to be at a place right now, where we cannot seem to find the bigger, more creative, and often obvious answers to some things. Or even know where to look for them because "normal" isn't normal anymore. Maybe it never was, but it sure felt that way. I know I long for something I can't even describe and I want to return to that "normal" as soon as possible to see if it was lost there somehow. But, let's face it, we never will. No matter what world, country, or personal events have happened in our lives, the outcome of any return to normalcy has always looked different, due mainly to the fact that in the process, we ourselves had changed as well. For me, the change that has happened I has caused me to be less like my true self than at any other time in my life. I'm comfortable sharing that because so many others have shared that it is happening with them, too. I don't always feel "normal" and I certainly don't always respond that way sometimes.

It has been suggested that we have become polarized within ourselves, within our country and within the world as a whole. An atheist friend of mine admitted that we "could sure use that anticipated Christian Second-coming to happen now. Rome isn't burning—yet," he said –" but if there is a second-coming that will rescue us from any conflagration it needs to be now." He mentioned the potential, that according to some predictions, the second coming is imminent and will bring with it some kind of cataclysmic global explosion that could take us out of our confusion. If it doesn't happen, he suggested that we might end up on a bed by the window trying to figure out life in all its chaos and confusion at this point in time. A little dire, I admit, but laying in bed longer in the mornings sometimes, while pondering what the day could look like, feels a bit like that. He, and I are ready for something better. Maybe not all of you, but I'll bet some of you are

How do we start this return—both on a larger scale and then in our own personal lives? Thich Nhat Hanh suggests this rather radical approach for the larger scale of the world:

"The situation of the world is like this. People completely identify with one side, one ideology. To understand the suffering and the fear of a human being who thinks different, we have to become one with him or her. To do so is dangerous-we will be suspected by both sides. But if we don't do it, if we align ourselves with one side or the other, we will lose our chance to work for peace. Reconciliation is to understand both sides. Finding common ground may mean pulling the plug, as

mentioned in the opening humor bit, on the many places where we are stuck and and beginning again.

On the smaller scale of our personal lives, these steps from an article titled "*How To stay Young*". (unknown)

- Throw out nonessential numbers. These include age, weight and height. Let the doctors worry about them. That is why you pay them.

- Keep cheerful friends. The grouches will pull you down.

- Keep learning. Never let the brain idle. Do whatever to keep it active. And idle mind will atrophy.

- Freedom unused will also atrophy so allow freedom to flourish everywhere.

- Enjoy the simple things. Laugh often, long and loud until you gasp for breath.

- Let the tears happen Grieve and then move on. He only person who is with us our entire lives is us. Be ALIVE while you are alive.

- Surround yourself with what you love. Your home is your refuge.

- Cherish your health. If it is good, preserve it. If it is unstable, improve it. If it is beyond what you can improve, get help.

- Don't take guilt trips. Take a t rip to the mall, to the next county, to a foreign country—but, not to where guilt is.

- Tell the people you love, that you love them at every opportunity you have

On the days when none of this works, then go ahead, take that bed by the window, (be sure there is a window to look out of), pull the plug on all that stuff inside and let it drain out quickly until all is clear. No need to hang on to anything. Then let yourself be filled with Spirit's Love. When full, call up someone, or tell someone in person that they are loved. Bet you will hear the same back from them. People need to hear it.

My bed is by a window and tonight, weather permitting, I will be able to see the full moon. So reassuring in its constant cycling. I may go outside and let it shine down on me as I have a treasure in my heart that needs a blessing of reassurance.

From the window of Life.

Sherry

A PLACE IN THE CHOIR

The lyrics go something like this: "All God's children got a place in the choir. Some sing low, some sing higher. Some sing out loud on the telephone wire and some just clap their hands or anything they got."

Those words floated into my head and kept resounding over and over today as I took myself away from laundry, clothes that need mending, a deck that needs sweeping and other various chores, and headed out to spend some time in what could be the last of the warm sunny days of Autumn. I didn't know where I was heading, but as the words clamored to stay in my restless thoughts, my car, that likes to head in a certain direction, took me to one of my favorite places—the park. I would have preferred the coast, but that was obviously not meant to happen, so I let that go because the sun was not to be wasted. Never waste a sunny day is my motto, and from the looks of the clutter in my house, it could also be my theme song.

During the 4 ½ hours I spent in the park, a lot of "God's critters" showed up to assure me I am not alone in the world, even if it feels like that sometimes. I was blessed to interact with over 50 ducks, of various kinds, as they came to see if I would share my chicken wrap with them. They let me know their disappointment in my being totally selfish with my food. I guess they can't read the sign that says it isn't good for them. Or maybe they just choose nor to abide by the rules. I get that as I'm like that sometimes.

After the ducks came two squirrels, a parade of various leashed dogs, their two legged owners, enough bicycle riders to host a race, a baby goat on a leash (yes-a goat), and a baby kitten being carried by a very sweet little girl. At the playground there were children of all sizes, cultures and abilities, including a sweet boy with a brace on his neck in a motorized vehicle that circled the sand pit. An elderly couple was celebrating an anniversary with family members present—all masked. Behind them was a young man training a leashed hawk. On a slight knoll a Native American young man with long air held in place with a headband and no shirt, sat chanting softly, shirtless in the warm sun and then sat silent for a long time with closed eyes. I got to exchange some greetings with him when I went to my car. I had a short conversation with a fisherman and a woman with a strong British accent.

On a day like this—yes I was masked the whole time—I realize that a gathering place such as a park, serves as a connecting point where people can come together to distance in fresh air, see life untouched by politics, a virus, and other distractions of the world we are living in. Everyone I met nodded and exchanged words, stepped out of the way as needed, and let themselves just be who and what they are. Same freedom for the other beings of God's natural world. The magnet of the outdoors is always there for God's critters and the many souls who raise their voices in honor of the joy of participation in the choir. Even the trees could not stop singing and their leaves moved and fell in their own rhythm.

Soon we will have to sing our song in the more confined, heated and sheltered world of our homes and I want to say something inspirational, helpful, profound or even entertaining, but words just aren't there, except for the words to the song still spinning around in my head. We all have a place in the choir, so let's not stop singing our song. Sing it loud and clear in any way available—electronically, from the front porch, on the phone, rolled down car windows (distanced of course), whatever- however we can find. This little three-liner came in the mail yesterday in a card and I think it fits here:

- *If you see someone falling behind, walk beside them (sing their song with them)*

- *If you see someone being ignored, find a way to include them. (create a new melody)*

- *Always remind people of their worth—one small act or word of affirmation could mean the world to them. (Help them write new words, or write new words along with them).*

Our choir may be a bit scattered for now, but when it returns and we can be together again, "what a day for rejoicing that will be." Those words are from a song in an old hymnal from my childhood that I pulled out from a box in my shed so I could re-introduce my fingers to the keys on the new piano that is now in my living room. The door was open when I played that song and the neighbor's dog let me know he was singing, too. All creatures got a voice in the choir—and so do you. I hear you! I Love your song.

Happy singing! Tell the world all about you because you are part of God's choir every minute of your life.

Singing in the park—as often as I can.

RAINBOW SHABBAT

In honor of the possible feast for our world
And the table will be wide, and the welcome will be wide.
And the arms will be open wide to gather us in.
And our hearts will be open wide to receive.
And we will come as children who trust there is enough
As we come unhindered and free,
And our aching will be met with the wine of life.
And we will open our hands to the feast without shame
And we will turn to each other without fear,
And we will give up our appetite for despair
As we taste and know the delight.
And we will become drink for those who thirst,
And we will become the blessing,
And everywhere will be the feast.

—Poem by Jan Richardson

ANT POWER

As I laid the soup spoon on the counter, I noticed something very small moving across the corner heading toward the dish rack. It was a very small sized triangular shaped piece of spinach and it was moving at a fairly steady pace. Then all of a sudden it teetered, stopped moving, and out from under it came a very small ant. Fascinated by the apparent strength of such a small creature, I decided to see what it would do next.

Much to my surprise it re-entered where it had come from and then came out again and began to try to move the piece of spinach once again. It looked like it might succeed, but it didn't. So it crawled back on again and went about one third of the way around and tried again—twice. That attempt failed as well, but not the determination of the little determined ant I named Jimmy, in honor of an ant story I have on tape told by Garrison Keillor. So I spoke to Jimmy, encouraging him to not give up. I don't know if he understood, but with all the determination of a child who sees a dish of ice cream within reach, Jimmy went to another corner of the leaf fragment and tried again. He was able to push it a tiny bit forward.

I assumed he was about to give up his prize, which he might have been trying to take back to his family. Then I realized he had another plan in mind. Out from under the tray of my dish rack, came two other ants heading in Jimmy's direction. Evidently he had called out for help, or maybe they were watching to see if they were needed. In any case, they all took positions around the leaf and slowly the bit of leaf began to move in a direction that seemed to be determined by these plucky three.

At that point my phone rang. I had to leave the scene and go into the living room to answer it where it lay on my coffee table. I made a hurried conversation and said I needed to take care of something. I had to find out what happened with Jimmy and his friends, but I refrained from sharing with the office manager on the phone what I was up to—for obvious reasons. When I got back into the kitchen, Jimmy, friends and the bit of spinach leaf were gone. I looked everywhere I could think of, but it was definitely not in my sight. I will never know where they all ended up, but the perhaps silly little event did give me something to think about, besides the Frank Sinatra song that has lyrics referring to an ant and a rubber tree plant.

First of all, it seemed to me that Jimmy's heart was really into his task. He had a purpose and he stuck with his goal. Secondly, when he got into a difficult place with that task, he either called on friends to help, or they cared enough about him and his challenge to offer their services. Thirdly, the task was completed because of both the ability to stay with a task, and to ask for help, or be willing to receive it, when offered. What a beautiful visual example for our lives. Especially the realization that all forms of life have intelligence, purpose and the desire for a good, peaceful life, which is possible when we all work together.

MEANDERINGS TOWARD MEANINGFUL LIVING

A good and very wise friend said to me the other day, as I was verbally sharing and questioning what I might do next in my life—"Remember, life is a process, not an outcome". Somehow I had thought I needed to be more specific in response to friends and family members who seem to need to know what is up for me in my thinking and planning. I understand their interest and concern as some of them may be involved in caring for me as I move into the next decade of my life and they would like to have some idea as to how that would or could impact their lives, as well as mine.

To me that kind of thinking is about outcome, and I am still "in process"—perhaps naively so, but that is how I am and how I think. It is like wondering if and when you will feel fully "grown up" while being full of doubts as to whether it will ever happen. Until you realize "grown up" is best related to physicality, rather than to human nature. Jesus said "bring the little children to me, for such is the kingdom of heaven" and children are always in process. They are the outcome of love manifest and they enter fully unencumbered into that process, showing much delight in exploration along the way. Taking the hand of a child can draw you right into the happiness of participating in "process."

As people in process we look for deep meaning and purpose in a timeless quest that, while not being definable in the absolute sense, certainly keeps us busy and interested along the way because we think it is definable. Silly us. Meaningful living can happen at any age and therefore is not an outcome. It is, instead, a very entertaining, challenging and quizzical process that takes us through all kinds of actions, attractions, and distractions and can keep us very entertained, as well as humbled. Especially when faced with all the choices available to us as we meander along life's path.

My wise and good friend also reminded me that "there is one thing that can be more difficult than no choice, and that is too many choices." "So why does life keep offering us so many choices that are so confusing and difficult at times?" I queried. The answer was "It's inherent in the saying, Sherry— the opposite is NO choice. Is that what you would want?" Of course not. Especially since I'm not always that good at being obedient. Desirous of doing things with love, respect and caring, but not always "obedient." Thank goodness for our spiritual teachings which point how we can "hook-up" with a powerful Divine Spirit that will walk with us on our meanderings, through our choices, and on to the realization that meaningful living is and can be a part of our everyday life when we open to it and allow it to manifest.

I am grateful for the meanderings, the choices, the pitfalls and the successes, the teachings and the learnings, the ups and the downs, but most of all for the dear and lovingly supportive friends that surround me every day. Without them, life would have no substantial meaning.

THE ART AND PURPOSE
OF SELF-LOVE

Thumbing through a music book I bought on my first visit to Unity Village, I came across a song title "I Love Myself the Way I am." I had to smile at the title because when I was growing up, using the phrase "I love myself" would have brought scowls of disapproval, remarks about being egocentric or arrogant, along with reminders that only through admitting we were imperfect and in need of forgiveness, could we be considered even worthy of God's love. We were taught to love God first, our neighbors second, but never to look in a mirror and say "I love you self." The first time I had to do that in a spiritual grown workshop, I found myself totally unable to stare at myself in a hand held mirror for the allotted amount of time, much less able to utter the words of love to myself. I also had no real concept of what that meant.

To the contrary, it was quite easy to look at other people and tell them I loved them. It was especially easy with those in my family—my husband, my children, my parents, etc. and the children I had in my classroom when I was teaching. Easy because I knew they loved me. Beyond that, I rarely used the word "love." It was not that I didn't care about others, because I did. It was because when the love word was used in my family, it was not used casually. It meant something deeper and more personal. We signed letters to family and very close friends with the word "love" but otherwise, more common phrases were used.

I suppose one might think that kind of upbringing fostered the belief that someone had to be worthy or meet expectations or certain conditions in order to be loved. While that was not true entirely, it did set some limitations on how wide the heart was allowed to open to give and receive love. However, setting limitations on the human heart does not always work. Love is not something one can stop from happening. It comes when it comes and we either accept or allow unfulfilled expectations to hold us back from establishing truly loving connection with others.

That is also true for how we view ourselves. We set expectations and when we don't live up to them we are disappointed, depressed, embarrassed or filled with a whole set of emotions that make it very difficult to accept ourselves just as we are. We often say to ourselves "I could love you more 'self' if you were only prettier, thinner, taller or shorter, less bald, less wrinkled, more chic or graceful, looked more like so-and-so, had a better smile, was more talented, and on and on." What we fail to realize is that these perceptions are unfulfilled expectations that draw us inward, limit us in daily life activities and experiences, and can keep us from letting our hearts open to truly loving connections with others.

I know, you are probably wondering if I can look in the mirror yet. Well, let's just say that I'm still working on that one, especially as I age. I'm not quite sure who that person is in the mirror, but that white-haired, older woman has been loved and will continue to love—in all its forms. Love makes the world go 'round as the song says. Let's keep the circle going.

FINDING A PLACE
TO LAND

There it goes again…first in a straight line to the intended place and then suddenly it shifts direction. After the shift, multiple directions for travel present themselves and I have a hard time deciding where to land. It makes me think of that saying "when you come to a fork in the road, take it." I immediately get a remembrance of the photo that often accompanies that saying. It is a photo of a table fork with four or five one-directional pointed projections on it. "Which one is the most important," I ask myself. Which direction is a person supposed to go in that instance? Then, as I continue to ponder, "It" takes off again and, as I observe "its" rapid meanderings I become exhausted. I have to pause and sit for a moment because I just can't keep up with the pace.

In case you hadn't already surmised, I am talking about my mind. That amazing container of many years of experiences, adventures, names, decisions, dates, colors, thoughts, etc. etc. and still possessing the energy to race around like the Energizer Bunny of Ever Ready fame. Non-stop. What a marvelous, resilient, adaptive and yet confusing aspect of our humanness that, even though it is of utmost importance in determining our existence, it has no form that can be photographed and displayed on a Xray screen or captured in a piece of art created by the most masterful of artists. It is so important that, along with our bodies, it must be given enough rest to keep it from shattering into a thousand fragile pieces reminiscent of fragile glass. The creator provided this nebulous vehicle for our use, but like our invisible essence of Spirit, kept its shape and substance a formless mystery.

Tied to this enigma without shape, are other nebulous forms which we have labeled emotions and reactions, and thoughts, all of which follow a pattern in expression—many in split-second steps. We may not see the movement from one moment or step to the next, unless we pay careful attention. See if you can spot these steps in your experience:

- A thought arises

- A feeling follows

- Physical experience manifests (you may feel a sensation of heat throughout the body, a quick pulse, a face flush or a slight tremor)

- You then act upon that thought

Because this pattern happens thousands of times a day, it is very important to find a time to provide a place for our thoughts to land so we can be the healthiest, happiest and most whole of persons. A good landing pattern includes spending at least fifteen minutes a day in quiet reflection. Medical science has shown that doing this consistently can reduce blood pressure and therefore, the need for, or strengths of medicines prescribed for blood pressure, as well as helping us make better, happier and more success-ful decisions.

I have a good friend from whom I have learned the importance of just getting still, for a few minutes every day, no matter where, to practice the art of caring for mind and body in this way. The time is not structured or guided by any particular form of so called meditation, but in the stilling of the mind, along with letting it slowly wind down with some visualization, decisions have been easier, life less frustrating and enjoyment of life in general enhanced. I think of it as "a heart-healing experience."

Now—there it goes again—that silly multitasking mind of mine—taking off on its own and reaching for my shop-ping list while I send this essay off for editing. After shop-ping there is a medical appointment and then…see what I mean? Who's in charge here?—ha ha. I'll be ready for that 15 minute refresher for sure.

A PEARL OF WISDOM

M rs. Pearl B. Heath. The very name caused a buzz in the hallways leading to the art department of my undergraduate college. We called her Pearl B. behind her back, while raising our eyebrows in the knowing that when we were in her presence we must say "Yes, Ma'am" and address her as Mrs. Heath. And, from that point any undisciplined behavior of any kind was not tolerated. It took us until half way through the year to let our spines soften a little when she entered the room and to begin to realize that we were her world and that she loved us more than we thought possible. Some of us had talent, some of us didn't, and yet she had to get us through our first class of art fundamentals and with that in mind she rigidly led us, with a bit of manageable fear through what we needed to know to pass that required teacher preparation course. When we were done, she let us know how proud she was of us, and then over tea, let us know all the things she had learned about us individually and gave us guidelines for our future success.

One of those guidelines was—I wrote it down—"You know what your special gifts are and you know what you should and should not be doing with your lives. You had that planted in your minds and hearts when you were born. Some of you need not take an art class again—it's not your gift, but I want to see you in person at least once a term to see how you are doing with your other talents. And now I'm off to Italy. (or some other place in the world). My compass says it's time to head there this time."

How did she go there? Not East, as one would normally do, but she went West. That gave her the opportunity to have Italy as the goal, but enough stops along the way in various places to make the trip interesting. When she wanted to go to Japan, she headed East so she could do part of Europe on the way, but her goal was Japan. She got around the world 5 times this way. I have a little pearl box from Korea she left me in her will. Inside was a folded paper that says "You have what it takes. Now do it." She never forgot us or we her.

Why do I share this? Because she opened me to a new way of thinking and pursuing what my heart was telling me to do in life and I want to honor her wisdom, though she is probably driving her antique car around heaven somewhere now, making sure everyone and everything is in the best of order. (She was the first woman to have a car on campus back in the 30's. She thought it very practical.)

1. The only way to navigate life is to know yourself and trust yourself and then you will know how to proceed.

2. Reflect on successes and evaluate mistakes.

3. Follow your instincts because that's your jewel box of wisdom.

4. Set the intention and then take action. That will keep you upright in any storm.

5. Find your faith and let it guide you. Prayer is your channel to receive input from God.

6. Make an agreement with yourself to not live your life to please others or do things that are not right for you just because you are afraid of letting someone down.

7. Have solid, upright expectations for yourself, and for others and love them into their highest potential. Just never be arrogant.

8. Take time out to travel, to learn new things, to meet new people and to do things with your hands.

CHANGING THE
EQUATION

He looked me straight in the eye, right in the middle of my high school algebra class and, absolutely quite upset with me, said for all to hear, "I can only say to you, Miss Ripple (that was my maiden name)…I can only say that I hope and pray you will never have to teach math, of any kind, above the 5th grade level when you get out in the field." I hoped so too, because I never was good at math, or arithmetic, as it was called when I was in grade school. Numbers just got jumbled in my head and floated off into some kind of vortex when I got beyond the traditional add-subtract-multiply-divide construct.

Words were another thing. They came together in correct spelling and formation without much bother. Try to blend the two—numbers and letters—and make sense out of it, was not something my mind could handle and it was very obvious as I attempted to navigate through my required high school Algebra class. But still, I sat there stunned, not due to the fact that I was in agreement with him, but that he would point that out in front of my peers. He stormed out of the room and I became frozen in my seat.

In the stunned silence that followed his exit, with my body beginning to shake from held back tears, I got up out of my seat, took the chalkboard eraser off its tray and began erasing everything on the board, beginning with the day's date. Soon I was joined by one classmate and then another and soon we had erased the entire board and begun to throw erasers at each other. This was followed by paper airplanes, and other various things that sailed easily through the air until we were all completely dissolved into laughter and totally out of control. And, I had started it all.

The consequence? Nothing. Yes, absolutely nothing. He walked back into the room, saw the mess, saw all of us standing there with spent energy and proceeded to the chalkboard and wrote two page numbers on the board and the following words: "You have 1 hour to complete this work and hand it in. You will work in absolute silence. Now get to work."

On graduation day he came up to me, took my hand to shake it and said words I have never forgotten. "Miss Ripple, I should have suspended you on that day, but it was the first time I had ever seen you really let go, let it all out, quit being so controlled and self-contained. I saw spirit in you I had never seen, but knew it was in there. I saw you laughing your head off, in leadership of a bunch of rowdies, and letting me have it for being so hard on you, which I deserved. You are now ready to go out into the classroom. You can teach from that place of the true you. Remember to set expectations, take charge when needed, tell it like it is for you and make laughter a part of all you do in the classroom and in your life." And then he added, "Stay loosened up. It becomes you—but just don't ever try to teach math beyond 5th grade level. Promise me." I kept my promise.

This event taught me that when you are being authentic, when you change anger into laughter, when you can allow others to feel your pain and when you can acknowledge theirs, together you can be a part of the healing of the world. When you can be forgiven by someone for being out of control and offer that forgiveness in return, you will also learn to be a part of the change that is possible. Life is hard at times and when it is, that is the time to look for what I call "the rose people"—those who clearly see the rose of potential and not the thorns of human imperfections, those who are ready to help you along the path and are willing to do what it takes, even if it's risky, to help that happen. Seek them out, or better yet, become a "rose" person. Be wise, but also be brave when it comes to helping others find joy in their lives. We can't do the work all by ourselves. We often forget how to have joy along the way. We need to be set free to allow the light and joy to come in—the joy that comes from finding and being our true selves and helping others find their authenticity.

When I graduated from college my Algebra teacher was there. At my 25th high school reunion, he was there. The way he taught me about life may seem cruel, but he knew me at a depth I had not comprehended and he cared enough to throw me headlong into uncharted waters, knowing I could swim if I wanted to. This was the time for me to make that decision. Maybe it was Spirit working through my teacher and using what has been referred to in some literature as the 2x4 approach, but had you known me at that time you would have known how much it was needed if I was going to move on in my life.

Yes, I drove my teacher to frustration, but what he did made all the difference in my 30 year teaching career. Some of my classmates are still on the planet and remember the day. We have laughed about it more than once. We still wonder how he was able to do what he did for each of us, in his own very unusual way, which would make several other good stories.

These events occurred at a time when I covered up my feelings of inadequacy with a rather self-assured persona that my teacher saw through. He saw something in me that needed shaking up and took the risk of a bold step to break the shell of my resistance to admitting, not only to math not being my strong point, but that I was holding back in participating fully in the things I was good at. As he told me later, "I wanted you to teach from your strengths and if you did, math would take care of itself in surprising ways, which it did through my students and their parents. That is another story.

In order to let the light into the dark places we have to open the door, allow a wall to crack a little, allow our defenses to fall and then grasp hold of the truth of our Divine self. In most philosophies, that is stated and a letting go into a higher power. From there we need to move forth into reaching out our hands and hearts to others, be there for them, support and love them, walk with them along with them in their journey. This is like changing an equation in human expression that can bring balance and hope. Let's do our work—maybe not so harshly, but definitely with ourselves strong in the belief of our ability to be a part of change—and definitely with Love.

A STORY OF REMEMBRANCE

While a friend and I were walking through a downtown alley way on the way to the car, we found ourselves unable to avoid hundreds of acorns covering the walkway, partially hidden by a soggy blanket of very wet leaves. Though many had already been crushed, there were enough left under our shoes, making audible sounds of resistance to being stepped on so deliberately. At one point I stopped to just look at them, feeling as if I should perhaps offer verbal apology for disturbing them. I then picked up five to bring back home with me. I wasn't sure why I did that, but now that they have dried off and are sitting together by my small desk lamp, I realize they have a story to tell. A silent, and very short story, but a story nonetheless.

Each acorn wears a hat of the same design and almost the same size. Under each hat, however, there are "bodies" of various shapes, widths, lengths and shades of color. None of them look like their host "parent"—the tall, oak tree from which they came. Yet they will, in time and under the right conditions, reproduce themselves as a visibly identifiable member of that plant species. They will have completed their life cycle with not too much fuss and bother.

Like the acorn, we human beings come into our life cycle in various shapes, widths, lengths and shades of color. Our hats differ from the acorns however, in that ours are displayed in different hair colors, influenced by our inherited DNA. Like the acorn though, we too are part of a life-cycle and we have a purpose for being who and what we are. Unlike the acorn, we tend to spend a lot more time trying to figure out what that purpose is. While we ponder, the acorn just gets on with the business of becoming a tree again. No questions asked.

How easy life would be if we were able to move through our lives like the acorn—unencumbered by all the things that impact us and cause us moments of confusion about the eventual outcome. But life for us is not designed that way. Unlike the acorn that just falls where gravity takes it, we have the options to determine where we want to land, how we plan to get there, and who we will allow to join us on our journey. The result of that divinely provided privilege is that we form attachments to both the outcome and the companions who join us on the journey. Because of this, and the length of our lifespan which differs from the little acorn, we become vulnerable to a kind of roller coaster of emotions at times, including those of joy, love, fear and grief, to name a few.

We begin the month of November with a focus on the experience of grief. Events throughout the world, in our own country, and in our church have impacted all of us, stirring up questions about life, about purpose, and how to respond spiritually to these various events—as well as how to move on and find the good in all of it.

To this experience of shared grief, I offer these thoughts gleaned from some of my reading: 1) Sorrow can change us for the better if we allow it to do so. We don't know how, but we do know it changes us forever. 2) An important part of our response to our grief is to name it, honor it and learn to live in its shadow as we continue to live out our lives to the best of our ability. It does not serve us to stuff it away in the hope it will disappear. Our growth is dependent on our learning to walk through the dark places and out into the light. 3) Part of our response must be to find some small measure of healing through taking action, preferably by offering comfort, reaching out to others in willingness, assist with what is needed, encouraging the re-establishment of hope, and the offering of pure and unconditional love for each other, no matter the circumstances.

As I offer prayers for peace, I know that in your hearts you will join me and together we can make a difference, even if it's here in our small community, where we have been planted to grow into and become tall oaks of human expressions of the Divine.

EVER NEW

A relaxing afternoon visit to a beautiful, peacefully flowing river nearby brought, not just to mind, but also deeply to the heart, a renewed sense of wonder at the way nature can sustain, nourish, and call forth the most beautiful responses from our very soul. Even in all the goodness of the days of the past week, the mind and body desired a change of scenery and from the pace of the routine I can so easily fall into. The sound of the smoothly flowing water, the smell of the grass beside the river's shoreline, the gentle breeze from lush green trees, and the warmth of the summer sun delivered, as always, a peace beyond understanding. It reminded me of the words in the 23rd Psalm where it talks about being led beside still waters where soul is restored. True, the river was not still, but it brought a kind of stillness to my whole being. I was wonderfully refreshed and renewed. Most likely you have experienced this many times as well, whether it be in our Oregon of gentle summers or other places of beauty on the planet.

What I was not prepared for, however, was the poignant reminder of how many years of my life have gone by already. Sometimes I so easily forget my age, even with the use of the walker I carry around with me these days. There also arose an internal swelling of the desire and determination to begin right now, to continue throughout the remaining days of my life, to ever refresh and renew that life—daily, weekly, monthly, yearly—by saying yes to every opportunity that arises that will take me out of myself, my surroundings, my thoughts, my fears, my narrow thinking, my daily routine, or anything that stands in the way of my continuing to learn, to experience, to grow. I have, at times, let myself feel limited by the physical manifestations of my aging process and said no to things I really wanted to do. No more.

The experience of the visit also reminded me that there are many ways to go down a river. Sometimes you get to physically ride on the raft or in the boat, sometimes you can float or swim, sometimes you can watch others and pretend you are on the device with them, and sometimes you can travel in your mind while you visually enjoy its beauty. Even that can be so very rejuvenating and refreshing. And, you don't have to be on the river to understand it's message or take the journey. There is always visually taking in its beauty from the shore— or imagining it in your meditation time and receiving the message it has for you, especially if being actually in or on the water is not your "thing".

Now, though it takes place in another part of the world, and is entirely unrelated to the river experience, a video I received that touched me deeply reminding me of the many things I have yet to learn about, to experience, or participate in vicariously, that can bring newness and freshness to my life. In this video, I was reminded of four things that I do not think about on a daily basis and so they felt new when I became aware of them: 1) a piano can be played and useful anywhere in the world, including a jungle—we can reach the soul of one of the most beautiful animals on earth through sharing the music, or any other creativity we have within us—2) there is always a way to be and feel useful in life, and 3) "seeing is believing" is only one half of a whole truth because there are many ways to experience truth and beauty and healing. So Many ways to refresh mind, body and soul. Many ways to bring our gifts and energies to the world that can help us stay fresh and new as individuals.

LOVE IS LIKE A LAKE
FILLED WITH LILIES

There is a story told about a particularly beautiful lake covered entirely with exquisite water lilies and as the people pass by they stare in wonderment and exclaim in delight at its beauty. It is as if they had been given a special gift, for the covering of the once bare lake top seemed to have happened over night. Surely it was a blessing from a most generous God and something to be treasured.

What they did not realize at that time, was that a wise person in the village, wishing to add something of beauty to the area around their village, had on a spring day, planted one water lily on the lake, knowing that one water lily would grow to many because the number would double each day. The lilies took 30 days to cover half the lake. On day 31 the entire lake was covered. This is called the law of doubling.

Love can be like the lilies, if we are willing. One expression of love, either in word or deed, has the ability to double and spread to the far corners of many hearts, changing the landscape of existence exponentially. Love, like music, has been confirmed as something inherent in human response systems with the power to transform human experience regardless of culture, ethnicity or gender. And yet, we tend to interrupt its flowering, plucking its buds, negating its potential to manifest in our lives both personally and globally; perhaps because we don't fully understand yet, that the cost of not loving is far greater than what we would have to let go of to allow love fill the lakes of our hearts and of the world.

I remember, often, how one of my first grade students taught me love's lesson. I was pregnant with our first child, experiencing morning sickness and trying to keep a classroom functioning at the same time. I had many grumpy days and on one occasion lashed out at this adorable young child over something I look back on now as trivial. He put his head down on his desk and cried and then looked up at me, with tears on his gorgeous, dark eyelashes and said "I love you anyway." In that one moment, like the 31st day at the lake, my heart filled from shore to shore, with such incredible warmth that I knew this child was my teacher of love. Consequently, perhaps, it was my last time ever of morning sickness. "I Love you anyway" expressed through speech or action could unpollute the lake of our existence and cover it all, everywhere, with the fragrance of sweetness and peace. Don't you think?

SURPRISED BY JOY

I have a confession to make. I have to make it because I seem to have projected a false image out into much of the world and it keeps coming back to haunt me. Not in the form of ghosts or visions or raised eyebrows, but in the things people say to me like "I so envy your faith and how you chose a goal in life and went for it in spite of everything"—or—"To know what you wanted to do in life and to make it happen is really an inspiration." My favorite is: "You are such a role model for women of today." I am? Really? Gosh, I never had that in mind at all. I am just someone whose life has required much independent action from me. Fortunately that just happens to match my internal hard drive.

What I truly am is a wanderer; in my mind, my pursuits, my interests. In other words, I tend, when something interests me, to pursue it until I am tired of it, got what I needed from it, feel blessed by it and then I am on to the next thing. Often that "next thing" is the result of a door that the previous "thing" opened and I happily hopped through it for the next exploration into something new and different. I am not one that tends to choose the most predictable or safest way.. Well, not until I turned that magic age of 70, that is, and had to pay more attention to an aging body.

The fun part of this wandering is that the inevitable fork in the road, showing up when least expected, often offers me two really good choices. While I may have wondered about "the road not taken," the one I did choose always turned out to have all the offerings of good, bad, ugly, beautiful, precarious and challenging things my soul needed for its growth along with pain, joy, fear, wonder—you name it. Life is like that, it seems, while we are in this form. Someday I will know what it's like in another form, but not yet.

What is true, however, is that I do not wander without purpose. I am always interested in staying as close to God as possible and being surrounded by the protection and joy of that ever-present energy of love. C. S. Lewis, author of that amazing series, "Chronicles of Narnia," and dozens of other books said: "You must not even try to do the will of [the Father] God unless you are prepared to know the doctrine of what it means to [be totally overcome by joy.]

Immersed in the act of wandering I am always unprepared for the joy of it all, but in the end of each wandering, when something new is discovered, piercing through my resistance, forcing me to change at some level, joy is always present. Profound, amazing, awesome, it shows up, whether I am in a classroom, on a walk, on the beach or the stage, with family or in front of a congregation, even in a grocery line—in the most unexpected moments I am truly surprised by the joy of the adventure. It has been said that joy is the sign of the Presence of God. Unearned—Grace in its unfathomable offering. Thank you, God.

HOME

The patchwork quilt was stretched tightly on the wooden frame set up in the living room of Mrs. McKee's house, there was a fire in the wood stove and a chicken roasting in the oven. As I walked through the door, I was greeted with such warm smiles and lots of questions, all blurted out at once—fingers of the four women's hands still poised to make the next stitch on the piece of homespun art they were creating.

"How does it feel to be done with the first quarter of your school year? I'll bet those 5th graders tired you out plenty." And, "I hear June will be your wedding month. Have you and Bob picked out the date yet?" Followed by other inquiries into what they each had been probably talking about before I came, wondering what I would say.

I answered as many as I could, feeling my concerns about the rest of my life fading into the mists somewhere as I was enveloped by the warmth these women shared with me. "Oh, this feels so nice," I thought. Why would I want anything else other than to settle into the loving routine of this community that had nurtured me through my growing up process. It would have been so easy to "come home" and be a part of it. So easy. But I had other dreams and action plans I had put into motion and they called to me, too, at a deeper level. My path was waiting.

From this one experience, and a few others along the path of life, I have come to realize that truly, home is where the heart is—not physically, or mentally but spiritually. Like what I felt in that warm, cozy house that became a metaphor for me.

1. If I give out love and show interest in other people, there will always be smiling faces returning love, showing interest and concern, and caring about making me feel welcome no matter where I am. This has proven to be so true through the years.

2. The warm and cozy kitchen is made that way when those in it are remembering to love and accept people for where they are as they prepare food to nourish their bodies and souls. Everywhere from brick ovens in Africa and hibachi pots in Japan to state of the art American kitchens, the warmth of friendship, caring and acceptance can be nurtured.

3. The patchwork quilt was being created from pieces of left over cloth from clothing worn by young children, farmer husbands, wedding trousseaus, and other clothing pieces from life. It was being sewn together by a fundamental Christian, a devout Catholic, a Jewish Rabbi's wife, the wife of a Japanese farmer who had once been in an internment camp in Oregon, and someone who believed in God, mostly, but was not a member of any organized religion. Their hands delivered the threads of life to the whole created from the pieces.

4. The quilt represented, to me, the coming together of so many aspects of culture, life, personalities, etc. and was my first true realization of the oneness of all things.

Home—"How to always be at home" will be the topic of Jon's talk this Sunday. I'm sure he will say much the same thing, but I want to add these things as well: You can always go home again in your heart— wherever you are there are people just like you so relax and accept them as your own— love is always the winner— Spirit is always with you so you have nothing to fear—You can meditate in an ashram, by the ocean, under a dripping umbrella, and dozens of other places and thus carry "home" with you at all times. Or, you can choose to do none of these things and I can guarantee you that as you near the end of your life, going home in your heart will be the first thing on your agenda and you will end up doing those things anyway. SO why not start now.

You are my family, our church is my spiritual home, and I carry everything else in my heart and feel so blessed.

In love,

Sherry

Radiating

———❦———

"The flower doesn't dream of the bee.
It blossoms and the bee comes."

—Mark Nepo

ANOTHER VERSION OF THE CHRISTMAS STORY

In the late 60's I was teaching 3rd grade at the American International School in Tokyo, Japan and when Christmas came, because of the 17 different nationalities represented in my classroom, it was not the only holiday celebrated at that time. Still, because it was talked about on the school campus, I had my children write their version of either the Christmas story as they understood it, or about any holiday that they wanted to share with me. This following story is what one of my students, whose father was a minister of the Christian faith and whose mother was Japanese, handed in to me. I hope you enjoy it and that it will bring some lightness and laughter into this Holy Week.

"Mary and Joseph were on their way to Bethleham but when they got there, there was no place to stay. Not even at any motel. This guy told them about a barn down the road. They went there and it had hay in it and some cows outside eating their hay. Their donkey liked hay so they decided to stay there and the farmer said it was ok with him.

The farmer was trying to get all his sheep into the sheep barn but there was a noise up in the sky. It was angels singing and he liked that. The angels were just hanging around in the sky. One angel with a big voice told the farmer that a baby king was going to be born in his barn that night. So the farmer called up all his friends and told them to come over.

Then a bright star showed up in the sky so they didn't need flashlights to get there. When they went into the barn there was baby stuff everywhere...diapers and bottles and stuff like that. The dad was looking a little confused, but one of the farmer's wives brought sandwiches and potato chips and that made him feel better. The mother was making a blanket and she put it over the baby and he went to sleep. She was really pretty and she looked nice in her blue dress. It kind of looked like a bathrobe though.

The farmer told the others that it was a special baby that was going to be a king so everyone was quiet. The kids who came along were quiet, too. It was a special baby like Aaron, who is Jewish. (Aaron was in my class). I don't know how long they stayed in the barn, but my Sunday School teacher said they had to stay maybe a week because the baby had to be baptized. She said his name was Jesus.

Ny dad knows a lot about Jesus and I sing "Jesus Loves Me" when I go to bed."

Well, there you have it. If you want to check out the more accepted form of the Christmas Story, check out the Gospel of Luke, Chapter 2 in the New Testament. It's not very long, but I always have a special feeling of joy when I read it. Maybe it's because I had to memorize it as a child and be Mary in a Christmas play at my church a long time ago.

Maybe it's the music of the season, or the remembrance of how my family celebrated it, including waiting for Santa to come. Whatever it is, my heart is soft, my eyes a little teary, my hope for the future born anew in me. May it be born again in you, and in all the world, regardless of our faith, for we all need renewal, and peace, and hope and reawakening to our connection with the Holiest of Spirits from which we too, came to do what needed to be done in our lifetime.

Happy Christmas, Happy New Year., Happy Hannukah. Happy everything that this season brings around the globe. It is, after all, about the birth of Love, only Love, which is the most important thing of all.

HOPE, PATIENCE
AND BALANCE

———❦———

Three items of interest came across my desk this week and when I sat down to write to you, I could not decide which one to share, so I am sharing all three, in the hopes that each item will have some meaning for the reader at this time of transition in our world, and particularly in our country since this is where we have the opportunity, in this moment, to reshape and create what will become our future from this moment on. Perhaps you have seen these before, and if you have, perhaps something new and relevant will come into your awareness, as it did in mine.

First: Caterpillars and HOPE

Caterpillars are so interesting in that they are filled with transformational things called "imaginal cells" and most spectacularly transform from little bits of bug-like life into something of larger and completely different form and shape. The imaginal cells within them are the ones to help them to transform into the beautiful and harmonious butterfly. Each of us express certain qualities of imaginal cells. We are awakening to a new possibility. Using our power to create change, we are clustering—somewhat virtually right now—into a more coherent signal of Love. Be encouraged as our world, which is itself an imaginal cell, begins shape shifting into a more harmonious expression. Help us envision and embody behaviors and beliefs that will nurture a brighter, more beautiful future. Do this by staying HOPEFUL!

Secondly: The Buddha and PATIENCE

To paraphrase one of the teachings of the Master Buddha: When the upper becomes the lower and the lower becomes the upper; and the inner becomes the outer and the outer becomes the inner; when the male becomes the female and the female becomes the male, then shall we together, not separately, but as one, then shall we enter the Kingdom of Enlightenment. This takes courage, insight, fortitude, faith, determination, and the ability to achieve integration in our lives—and it takes a great deal of PATIENCE because such integration does not come easily in a competitive world. Yet, it is the path to wholeness and peace for all. Be patient. We can and will make it if we keep the faith, commit to the practice, and help each other along the way.

Thirdly: Anthropology and BALANCE

A friend sent me an article from our local newspaper written by Doyle Rice. Rice explains that the mass of all our planets human-produced materials exceeds the mass of all life on Earth and its biomass. In fact, the average amount of materials created by humanity every week outweighs the human population! Perhaps once we face reality and truly grasp these shocking figures, we will begin to take responsibility for getting things back in BALANCE.

Anthropologist Margaret Mead was asked by a student what she considered to be signs of civilization in a culture. Her answer was unexpected, She said that the first sign of civilization in ancient cultures was a thighbone that had been broken and then healed. She then explained that with a broken thigh bone you cannot run from danger. If pursued, no one, human or otherwise, survives long enough for the bone to heal.

A broken femur that has healed is a sign that someone has taken time to stay with the one who fell, has bound up the wound and either cared for the one with the broken bone where they are, or carried them to safety and aided in their recovery. Mead said, "We are at our best when we serve others. That is being civilized."

Reinforcing Mead's thought is this note I just received from my daughter: "If you break a bone, calcium forms at the break site. The calcium is very strong. Stronger than the bone itself which actually weakens during the healing process. During the healing process the membrane around your bone turns into bone and fills the gap where the break was. Eventually the bone heals back to its original strength. We, too, can be calcium for others. We can be strong while others are weak and need time to heal."

As we enter into a new era of history, that will gradually transform our fractured politics of today, may we with HOPE and PATIENCE remember the unstoppability of Divine Grace. May this inspire us to continue seeking BALANCE even amidst times that seem unsteady. With BALANCE we can move toward uncovering, acknowledging and practicing the support of our universal family—"all God's Children." We can begin to unify with Divine calcium of spiritual Love, compassionate outreach and caring. As these qualities merge with unconditional acceptance and universal forgiveness, we will form an ever-stronger union not only within our own country, but also around the world, in ways we have never known before.

God Bless America. And may America bless the world as we lead by example from our hearts and souls.

Living in as much HOPE, PATIENCE and BALANCE as possible. I know you are, too.

Love,

Sherry

TOUGH AND TENDER

When I was 6 years old I came down with Scarlet Fever. I remember the knock on the door of the small parsonage we lived in and the voice that said, "Here are your signs for your windows. They need to be put up now." It was at that moment that my grandfather, my grandmother and I went in to quarantine.

My mother was at work at J.C. Penney's and she spent the next two weeks at a friend's house. It was my mother's salary that kept all of us fed and housed. I'm not sure how she got the things she needed from the house, but after she and my father divorced and we moved in with her parents, we didn't have many material things so I assume she was able to manage somehow.

As we walk through another phase of this present virus epidemic, memories of that time in my life came back to me quite vividly. I remember the bed I was in, the flowers of the wall paper, the patchwork quilt, the sheets Grandma had to change daily and wash in the wringer washing machine that stood in a corner of our small kitchen. I also can remember the feel of the rather rough covering on the couch in the small living room where I got to go and lay when I began to recover. I remember missing my friend Ruthie who I played with almost every day.

What comes to heart and mind is how my grandparents

cared for me. They had been exposed to a very serious and contagious illness because of me, yet somehow, even while caring for me, they made it through without getting ill. My mother, who could not come home until I was well, was the youngest of their 12 children and, at 10 years apart in age, my grandparents were in their 70's and 80's already. Yet, they never wavered in their care and it showed up in ways I will never forget.

My grandfather, who was a man of few words, but deeply spiritual and soundly religious, said to me: "You be tough. Not fight-tough—stand up for yourself tough. You be strong. You trust God. He will care for you." Then, "You play piano in church when you get well. Then you can praise God and say thank you that way." (I had been taking lessons since I was five—one whole year—but could play hymns)"These were said with a German accent, which was his first language. As a minister of a small German church he preached in German as well as English. Then in the morning and at night he would sit by my bed and tell God about it all and what he expected. As someone who had walked across Germany to escape having to serve in the military when Russia invaded Poland, he knew how to be tough in order to survive, and to walk in snow when someone stole his shoes during that walk.

My grandmother was a small boned woman of 5' 2". She was not much of a talker, but she read to me, sometimes falling asleep in the rocker she pulled up by me bed. She hummed while doing dishes, wrangling with the old wringer washer, sweeping floors, etc. She didn't hum while scrubbing the bathtub, however—just puffed and looked grim. She also braided my hair, washed my face, helped me walk when I began to get better, and helped me get dressed with the clothes she made for me. I don't remember having store-bought clothes when young. She would also stroke my arm, and sometimes my face. There was so much caring in those touches. I miss them, even today. She also made sure I said my prayers before going to bed—on my knees, as was the custom in our house, unless you were older.

Tough and tender– both of them were that. In today's world we are being called upon to be both as well. I would add- strong. Tough means to keep from getting pushed around and protecting what is good when bullied, perhaps. Not a "toughie"—but well, tough. Tough can have a lot of tender inside it and when used in a positive sense, tough and tender create strong. Tender is important. Tender with each other, with the four-leggeds and all creatures great and small. Tough enough to be durable, strong enough to stand in our Truth and be there for others, and gentle enough to Love deeply. OH how we need all three right now.

I'm not sure how I will make it through the winter this year. I don't even have the words to help you with your challenges. But, even though I want to be somewhere else so much during the next few months, I will tough-it-out with you because you are "my people." I will be strong in my faith , if you will help me with mine. I will believe in you and our future together, if you will believe in mine. And, I will hold Love in my heart for you. God, however you know, name or express that Divine nature, is there to be with us, too. We will make it through.

This Sunday I will be talking about strength in our diversity and how it takes all kinds of people to make up the whole and how to have gratitude for that. I won't see you in person, but will picture you all in your chairs in my mind.

Many blessings.

Sherry

ON THE BREATH OF GOD

First, a quote from Hildegard of Bingen, followed by a personal story: *"There was once a king sitting on his throne. Around him stood great and beautiful columns ornamented with ivory, bearing the banners of the king with great honor. Then it pleased the king to raise a small feather from the ground, and he commanded it to fly. The feather flew, not because of anything in itself but because the air bore it along. Thus am I, a feather of the breath of God.*

And thus am I, as I walk among the feathers of God whose bodies and minds have left the sound and rational life, but whose inner spirits are alive with great understanding of their identity and integrity as people of value and worth. I'm speaking of my daily forays to visit my husband at his memory care center, where I now grapple with his move to another cottage due to his physical decline. The people in this cottage are mostly in wheelchairs, many need assistance with eating, some verbalize unintelligibly part of the day, and others sleep much of the time. Here, in this place I have feared, I watch caregivers give with love, compassion, understanding and humor to help keep their "feathers": afloat as long as possible. I wonder what these caregivers have that I don't. They are truly the breath of God in visible action. And I believe that among them, invisibly but profoundly, walk the mystics of the ages, like Hildegard, who said: "*God hugs you. You are encircled by the arms of the mystery of God.*" This can be said as well for those who receive their care.

Hildegard also said" "*Holy persons draw to themselves all that is earthly. The truly holy person welcomes all that is earthly.*" This can be a challenge, welcoming all that is earthly. And I am far from deserving to be called holy. But as I struggled and recoiled and wept at placing my loved one in such an atmosphere as described above, this thought of welcoming all that is earthly helped me see what was mine to do. Thank you Hildegard—I feel your presence. There is a healing in the gradual smiles of acceptance by those being cared for, in their reaching out to touch me and hold my hand, and in their eventual gathering around the table to watch and listen to be talking with others. A feather-like uplift is happening within me. The breath of God can't do its work if we keep the doors closed, so I have had to open mine.

May the breath of the Divine surround you and lift you up like a feather. And may you know—and accept—your holiness.

UNWRAPPED WITH JOY

T hey were kept in their assigned slot behind the folding oak doors of our 1950s style stereo cabinet by my tidy, organized husband throughout the years of our passion for what he called "the best of the very best." Of course, I'm referring to our 33 1/3 rpm record collection—some classic, some Broadway shows, some individual vocal artists and some big band instrumentals. A few tears fall as I recall such good times and the happy discovery of a first edition album from *The Sound of Music*. Bob called it *The Sound of Mucus*, not out of disrespect—he loved the songs—but because I always got teary listening to it, or watching the movie over and over. And here I go again: another hour wrapped in the past, especially my favorite song: "My Favorite Things."

When the movie first came out, Bob and I attended the first showing in our town and immediately bought the album. We also named our daughter after the star, Julie Andrews. Ours was "Julie Angela"—Julie of the Angels. In the movie there is another song that makes me smile: "How Do You Solve A Problem Like Maria?" How do you raise a daughter so that her gifts, her joyous innocence, her personality, her special expressions, her childhood laughter and potential tears of confusion when she bumps up against life's quirks become not problems, but gifts full of potential and opportunities for her to become the person she was meant to be? The Abbess in the movie had insights, along with deep faith, and acted upon those insights and intuition to turn what seemed like a problem—Maria trying to be a nun—into an exuberant life expression that still charms, enriches and inspires the world today. Could Bob and I make life for our daughter a rich, meaningful and joyous one? Would she have the strength to emerge as a butterfly from the various stages of her unfolding life? What would her story tell?

The same for our son, Jeffery Kyle, named from a character in the movie *Written on the Wind*.

(As you can tell, movies and music were very much part of our lives.) Both children, much to our relief, made it through the gauntlet of youth, through any negativity both outer and inner, that might have caused them to think twice about themselves and be less than they truly are. They have given us not only great joy, but lots of grandchildren and more experiences of unconditional love than we could ever have imagined.

That is, once again, my own personal reflection. I hope that you will take time to reflect on a fond memory or two, and find your contemplation a moment in which you realize that you are a special gift to the world, and any problems you face are only the congestion of the traffic on the road that is taking you to your perfect place. And that you have many traveling companions.

Through music, dance and the spoken arts, we can move beyond those events in our lives and emerge from restrictive thoughts while stepping forth into our full expression. From there, in joy and passion, we can share our unencumbered, true and special selves with the world—no strings attached. Just celebrations of the love we share because of who we are.

SIGNPOSTS AND GUIDELINES

As I watched the teacher and her adult helper accompany a group of very young children down the sidewalk and come to a stop at a corner, a small boy pulled his hand away from another and began to hurry ahead on his own. He was, of course, stopped by the adult helper who also pointed out the stop sign they were waiting in front of and helped back to his place in line. The teacher then pointed out a One Way turn sign to the children, and due to the fact that they did not move right away and there were more hand gestures, I assumed they were getting a lesson in traffic and pedestrian safety. I wondered what they would do when they got a bit further and ran into all the new temporary signs up ahead, placed there by workers who were doing some repair work. So many things to learn about getting around in this world.

It made me think of all the cautionary sign posts and guidelines these children had yet to face as they navigated the physical aspects of moving around in our city. As I've been driving around lately, and taking walks as well, I've come to notice all the new signposts springing up every-where, telling us which roads will be closed or open on which dates and even when to expect the next projects and projected changes in traffic patterns. It seems we can't progress in any direction anymore using our inner compass of remembrance of how to get somewhere. We are learning to move through mazes of all kinds and have become dependent on the language of words printed on all kinds of backdrops in order to assure safe arrival at our destination. It can be very confusing, which is probably why we breathe a sigh of relief as we cross over the city limit sign and head down a more open road.

I thought of how most of the children I saw will be taught new vocabulary words by learning what a sign says as a parent or other adult points them out to them. They will learn to recognize such words as: Stop, Yield, Danger, Use Caution, One Way, Do Not Trespass, Slow, Right Turn Only, No Parking, etc. We have a lot of warning signs, as well as directional ones, and have had to invent a GPS system to get us through it all as we often can't find our way through the maze that also includes already abundant and increasing amounts of traffic lights.

I wondered what these vocabulary words of caution and direction might be having on the subconscious minds of our children? Do they perceive them as helpful at their young age, or are they constantly wondering what possible harm waits for them if they don't follow "the rules"—until they understand the reason for them, of course.

I was complaining to my daughter about all the construction signs and changes that are affecting travel within our city. She reminded me that where she lives in Florida, driving anywhere, even in broad daylight, one's vision requires squinting and narrowing because the maze of signs, lights and six traffic lanes is like going through an unending maze and one has to pay impeccable attention every single moment behind the wheel. She was happy when a recent job change necessitated a move to a small town named DeLand where, interspersed between traffic guidance signs and features, the city brought forth a desire to keep life simpler and people smiling, by placing unusual signs in various places around the city. Signs such as an eternity symbol with "Infinite Clearance" underneath, and ones that say "Breathe," "All You Have Is Now," "Relax," "UR Ok" and a heart shaped sign with the words "One Way" on it, to mention a few. You can see some of them in the photo above.

I'm thinking it would be so encouraging, while we teach the other safety type words to our children, to be able to point out the DeLand kind of words on signs around Eugene. We could even put some in our parks, various places downtown, or in the lobby of buildings. Taking time to have a brief conversation with children about these words, or even just pointing them out with a smile, might instill some positive encouragement for them, as well as add smiles or moments of positive lightheartedness for adults. What do you think?

To paraphrase a saying by philosopher-writer St. Antoine Dupree, "What is essential can be taught first with the eye, then with sound..."—to which I add, "how this is done determines the attitude of the heart."

WHAT MATTERS MOST

O ur house on the farm where I grew up sat on the top
of a hill and overlooked part of a valley on one side
and higher hills on the other. It was not unusual for me,
between chores, homework, and other activities, to climb
up into one of the trees in our apple orchard and sit gazing
out over the land below. I could see the farmland stretched
for miles toward the small town three miles away where we
did most of our shopping. From this vantage point I could
experience the coming and going of the seasons. I can
remember wearing shorts and climbing barefoot during
summer season and long stockings and heavy coat during
the winter, but leaving my shoes at the bottom of the tree
so I could grip better.

As I looked out over the valley, even as a young child,
there was a feeling of awe that spread through my whole
being. I wondered how God, as I understood then, could
come up with all these things, make them so beautiful and
then take them away sometimes. I was attending a more
fundamental church at the time and God was given a lot
of power over everything, and we were reminded that it
was our sins that brought chaos and destruction upon the
world and in our lives. I wasn't fearful of God, but I kept
"Him" at a distance, unless, of course, there was something
I really wanted or someone I wanted to pray for. Then I

needed the presence to cooperate with me, or just take over and do "His" thing.

I did understand, however, that something much bigger than any of us had some kind of plan for all of this, but I certainly didn't know what it was or how, beyond gravity and weather, it all worked. Though I seemed to get glimpses, it has taken all these many years since to finally get to a point of acceptance that, as Susan Jeffers said so well, "While none of us understands the Grand Design, we can commit to using all our experiences, good or bad, as the building blocks of a powerful and loving life. Then it is, indeed, all happening perfectly."

Author and humorist Connie Willis wrote something that always makes me smile and feel lighter about each day spent working through the unfoldment of the Grand Design in general: "A Grand Design (always capitalized, which seems fitting) we couldn't see because we were part of it. A design we only got occasional, fleeting glimpses of... involving the entire course of history and all of time and space that, for some unfathomable reason, chose to work out its design with cats and croquet mallets and pen wipers, (and other interesting stuff), to say nothing of the dog...and a piece of Victorian artwork...and us."

In the end, for me at least, as I let the mystery be itself, what matters most is, as Buddha said "How well did you love? How well did you live? How well did you learn to let go?" I'm grateful he put Love first as that is important to me. I'm still having trouble with letting go, but in the meantime, I believe we are all doing our best—at least I'm trying. Trying to remember to let God live through me-us: G = gift...O = of...D = the Divine.

EYE OF THE BEHOLDER

While waiting for a taxi ride home from a medical appointment in a crowded downtown area this morning, I was perched on my walker outside the tall building just watching people go by, exchanging nods and smiles and noticing the beauty of the day, in spite of the cloudy gray sky. It always surprises me how friendly people in general can be when an older lady with gray hair is sitting somewhere, choosing to smile and greet as often as possible. Eugene still has that quality if we look for it, as do other places.

At one point, as I was looking across the street at a special noodle place that holds fond memories for me, a tall, good-looking younger man stopped to ask for a direction. As we were chatting, a disheveled, age-indiscernible woman, pushing a loaded cart with apparently all her belongings stuffed inside stopped a few feet away and watched us. I thought—oh dear, I think a request for a handout is coming my way. The young man glanced her way, then after thanking me for help and telling me to keep warm, walked energetically on his way. As the woman came my way I thought to myself "Don't mess this up, Sherry. This is someone's daughter, doing the best she can." (I learned this wonderful expression and outlook on people from a dear friend of mine and it has served me so well!)

As she approached me, I smiled and she smiled in return. When she got closer to me I saw that she had enormous, beautiful brown eyes obscured by rather scraggly hair, and smooth skin with a dark red birthmark on the left cheek. There was a photo attached to a ribbon she was wearing around her neck. We began a conversation, about all sorts of things, including our children. The photo around her neck was one of a young boy, about aged 9 or 10. She got quite misty eyed when telling me he and his parents were killed in a car accident two years ago and because she could not keep up rent payments she had to leave their house where she had been staying with them. She showed me the newspaper clipping that described the accident so I could know that "it's the truth and wants to stop being homeless and find a place soon." As she began to walk on, I, of course, reached for my purse, but she put out her hand and said "No way. No way. That was not my intent when I came to you. You just looked friendly and I haven't had anyone to talk to yet today. Your acceptance was so kind." What a beautiful moment, and experience.

Here I had perched, looking at the beauty of the leaves still falling, the handsome face of a young man, the beauty of the Asian couple that had walked across the street carrying noodles in large cups, an adorable baby in a stroller, and admiring a colorful, art-deco style jacket worn by a young woman, and then was approached by someone who did not look "beautiful" by most standards. This made me realize once again that beauty is truly in the eyes of the beholder and quite often is perceived, not from the visual experience, but from that within that is touched and opened to receive, experience and feel the feelings of love, acceptance, and the oneness of kindred spirit, no matter the outer wrapping.

It's the same sort of thing when viewing paintings or other works of art. Some will inspire, touch and even change lives because the person who is viewing it is touched at some level of their being; while others will walk right by it and not even notice, but will be attracted by something else.

Beauty can transform the ordinary into the sacred, that's true, but what is beautiful for one may not be beautiful for another and sometimes, "ugliness," in whatever form it might take, can provide a window on beauty as well. I think of the children's story and the eventual musical "Beauty and the Beast" in which, in spite of the perceived ugliness in the beast, the beauty of that being shines through and it becomes beautiful because of what is in the heart and soul and mind. When we hold those things as sacred, all things can become beautiful. Like the song, "Everything is beautiful, in its own way..."

May you accept your beauty, let it shine through, see it in others, and may every moment in time be perceived as one of grand potential for discovering the beauty in all of life. Mother Theresa saw the beauty in all the souls she ministered to. May we perceive the same.

THE MAGIC AND POWER
OF THE CIRCLE

An afternoon science discussion in a classroom ends up in a heated discussion and then a bit of chaos begins to emerge. One of the students goes to the teacher's desk and picks up the old fashioned hand bell sitting on the corner and rings it once. Silence. Twenty four students head for the rug area in the corner of the room and form one large circle with a smaller half circle on one side. The teacher joins them and instructs them to take a deep breath and close their eyes for a moment. When it is calm enough, she asks who would like to be the observer for the first part (the one who will ring the bell if they need to stop and breathe again) Then the teacher offers the opening statement, reminding everyone that there will be no "cross-talk". They already know that that means they would have to stop again and they can only sit still for so long. "Let's begin. Who would like to start?," the teacher asks.

Several hands go up and a few side comments are made. The teacher raises her hand, palm out, and it becomes quiet again. "We will go clockwise now, since that seems to be easier at this point." As she nods to the student to her left, all eyes are focused on the speaker, and the discussion begins. Everyone who wants to can speak when it's their turn or they can pass. There will be a second round if it is needed to get comments from all who wish to speak but are shy, or too angry, in the beginning, or wanting to wait until they hear what others are saying.

Outside of needs for immediate intervention by the adult in charge, this was the way I chose to handle disruptive behaviors or out of control responses in my classroom. Sometimes we sat in circle and put someone in the middle who needed to be assured of their worth by their fellow students, or someone who received an award, or made some changes in their attitude and a whole bunch of other things…including coming up with ideas of how to make our classroom, the school or our lives better. It took a lot of hard work to get there with this "modus operandi"—but the results were incredibly rewarding. We did not use a talking stick, or a bean bag heart after learning that some people have a hard time not playing with them too much and being distracted by the very fact they have to try hard to be still when holding them (Kids ☺)

As I reflected on this piece of my past profession, I was reminded of how, for centuries, people have naturally and successfully gathered in circles to either pass on information, solve problems, welcome new members, celebrate events, prepare for change or evaluate how things are going for various things that have surfaced and need attention… Villages in Africa, Native American camps, King Arthur's round table, ceremonies to celebrate the change of seasons, campfires at outdoor schools, families around a table, sharing in story telling…so many ways that coming together in a circle can facilitate the experience of peaceful solutions or experiences that enrich life. Circles seem to have a way of bringing peace, resourcefulness, inspiration and calmness into a scenario and fostering rising self-esteem in individual participants when they are drawn into this participatory process.

THE POLKA DOT
UNIVERSE

Look around you! How many circular things do you see? In order to organize our time and space, it seems we have created a lot of things with parallel line, corners, squares, rectangles and other shapes. I'm thinking of things like tables with corners, desks, beds, buildings, doors, boxes, signs, you name it. For so many things roundness is not the preferred shape; at least at some levels. Think about this for a minute, picture in your mind all the square corners you can think of. Feel, if you can, how your brain "feels" when you are picturing them. If you give it some thought, you will notice a definite "feeling" inside your brain.

Now, let's shift to round things—like the center of a daisy, a beach ball, cookies, the moon, the sun, a baby's head, an apple, an orange, a hug, etc. Can you feel a shift in the "feeling" inside your mind? Scientists have shared photos of brain changes when we shift from picturing square shapes to round ones. Science has also shown that everything in the expanse of the universe has "roundness" as its basic shape. This includes our planet. The things on it are not all round, of course, but the cells they are made up of are round-like in their shapes. Even a drop of water will return to its original roundness if let to sit for a minute or so. When a snowflake melts, it doesn't melt into a shape with corners. It becomes a drop of water with rounded edges.

A famous Japanese artist, Yayoi Kusama, who creates all of her art by using thousands of dots—a form of pointillism—says this about what she has learned from her experiences and observations:

"Our earth is only one polka dot among a million stars in the cosmos. Polka dots are a way to infinity. When we obliterate nature and our bodies into polka dots, we become part of the unity of our environment."

What she is referring to is the idea of "self-obliteration" in which the individual ego, which she associates with domination as being "subsumed within patterns of dots and networks to become at one with the universe."

What does it feel like to be a dot in the universe in which we travel through a space filled with tiny spots of light? Kusama feels that contemplating and experiencing this illusionary perspective offers a sublime experience that connects to many themes in life that are circular, such as the cycles of life and death and the seasons. Even black holes and quasars are polka dot shapes that magnify the effect of innumerable celestial diamond-like emanations.

Some famous artists, such as Seurat, and even Van Gogh at one experimental phase in his work, used tiny dots, arranged in various patterns and colors, to create life-like scenes on canvas. They showed that as dots make up the whole, they can determine what the whole looks like. Strangely enough, the smaller the dots the clearer the painting.

Some other interesting observations: 1) Just the mention of polka dots can produce smiles. Clowns know this. 2) Polka dots are a key element in tribal art of the bushman of South Africa. 3) In Polish, polka means little woman and in Spanish, they are referred to as little moons. Designers, however, have incorporated polka dots into men's clothing, recently saying that we all need to be able to experience the joy of the universe. 4) They can be seen as white at one place and black at others when out in space. 5) Polka dots on Minnie Mouse's dress were to produce smiles and help her appeal to both boys and girls. 6) In some cultures, dots are symbols of the supernatural.

I like to think of it this way—Since all dots, whether spaced apart or close together in our human eye, are really representations of the whole and we are each individual dots that make up that whole. In this construct we can rearrange ourselves and determine what the whole will look like at any point in time. As dots, we are the world—a family of different colored dots traveling through space and time together in the polka dance of life. Also, as dots are incredible points of light, we are also incredible points of light that can bless the world by illuminating the dark places until they are filled with the light, love and joy we have to offer.

The whole universe is doing a divine polka. Let's dance. Just for the fun of it!

Anticipating

"Anticipation is a gift. Perhaps there is no greater gift. Anticipation is born of hope. Indeed it is hopes finest expression."

—Steven L. Peck

THE TIMES THEY ARE A CHANGIN'

It's pouring rain outside as the yard care company truck pulls up in front of my house and two hearty young men get out, unload equipment and set to work, making the usual amount of noise with their loud equipment This makes no sense to me so, keeping plenty of distance, I step out onto my porch and ask them why they are here today. "To do our work," was the response. "In this weather?," I ask them. "It's part of the contract and our job and we need the money," I am told. Their employer is on another job. I tell them that I pay per month and they can catch up on another day. The young men are trying to just make their rent payments now and have been laid off from second jobs.

I go to put gas in my car. I don't want to do it myself because it's awkward since I use a walker. I ask the attendant to do it for me since my tank is on the opposite side of my car and we can talk at a safe distance. I also have handy wipes in my car for the credit card concerns. He is not very polite about it and so I have to be diplomatic and insist.

Then I try to reach my bank by phone because the business I need to get information about cannot be done through a drive-in window. The phone wait time is exactly 29 minutes and then they tell me I should use my app…I can't remember my password because I just got the app and misplaced where I wrote it down. Changing it becomes a huge task. And the days wear on, full of things that keep me from all the things I had hoped to accomplish during this time of isolation and have thrown me into the world of technology that I have resisted, and so do not like at all and do not think it is serving us well in the long run, even though it is helpful at the moment.

But they are so minimal compared to all the things that others are facing—many of them insurmountable in varied ways, all of which touch me at depth, all of which I want to solve, all of which I feel so helpless about.

Most all of you are facing similar things and, like me are having a very difficult time being in isolation, while longing for life as it used to be and knowing that once this is over it will not be the same ever again. Which might be a good thing in many ways. Sometimes it takes a blizzard or a flood, etc. to clear the air, bring people together, and point out the things that matter and what needs to change. If we could just make those good changes stick, right? One way that has come to me by email from a friend, I offer to you now. It has become my mantra and, along with the return to my Ki meditation practice (probably new word to most but something I learned from my doctor) has helped me begin to shift into a better physical and mental frame of mind.

The mantra is this: Just say thank you one thousand times a day. With every breath say thank you. While washing dishes say thank you. While scrubbing the toilet, or wiping surfaces say thank you. while on the phone begin and end with thank you. When feeling frustrated, angry, or tearful say thank you even if a four letter word slips in. It's ok. Spirit understands. I walked barefoot in the puddles on my deck this morning saying thank you and it felt so good. My feet understood and my body responded.

So many miraculous, wonderful and heartfelt things are happening within our spiritual community at Unity of the Valley. Angels in people form are moving about all over the place doing errands of love and caring, phone calling and emailing, showing up on decks with love offerings, holding virtual meetings to help with solving problems, and on and on. Say thank you for the ways in which we are led to make it through these times. Say thank you for each other.

THE MIRACLE OF
RESILIENCE

A little over 2 years ago, on a warm sunny day with not
a cloud in the sky, Bob and I participated in a special
flower potting event in the beautifully landscaped gardens
at his care facility. We both love geraniums, and he spot-
ted a small, but very healthy looking red one and, with the
assistance of a very patient caretaker/gardener, placed it in
the small pot that was provided. The pot had been painted
by one of the residents and was purple with gold trim and
it still sits in its smallness on the window sill by my kitchen
window where I can see it every day. Because it is small I
have to water it almost every day.

I did not think the slender, fragile geranium would survive, especially considering my tendency toward lack of attention to my houseplants, of which I have very few, and as a
result I find myself apologizing to them when I do notice their
drooping leaves begging for attention. I did talk frequently to
this one though, and asked it to please stay around longer than
it may have wanted to and was afraid to repot it because of
my fear it would not survive the replant, given its very tender
roots. So it stayed in the same pot and the very same soil.

Just a few weeks ago it presented me with its first red
blossom, surrounded by very small, vivid green leaves. It's

stalk is still miniature, but it stands upright with a kind of pride that continues to give me comfort when I remember the heart of the person who chose it while in the midst of his illness, and the strength of the hands that planted it.

Something in the heart of that stalk is speaking to me of the resilience of nature, even under less than perfect circumstances. I don't know if it would have spoken to me in the same way had it gone on to be a big, bushy plant like all the other geraniums on my deck. This little plant soul feeds me daily with its reminder of the life force within it and all of us, of the miracles wrought by collaboration between human and nature for mutual survival, and the beauty of the diversity of the outcomes that are possible when we care enough to live in harmony with, and pay attention to, what can be manifest by love and acceptance.

Perhaps the planter, now on the other side, is caring for it as well. I can't know from here, but I choose to believe that he is, and therefore reminding me that even in the small things there is hope. And, if we shift our thinking in the direction of believing that miracles are still possible in these shifting times, we can one day see the world blossoming before our very eyes everywhere and flowers rising out of those places where the seeds of love and possibility thinking were planted, supported by faith in the one Creator of us all.

WHAT'S AROUND
THE CORNER

A good friend and I share a passion for investigating new things. One of the "things" we enjoy is taking drives on quiet afternoons and investigating side roads we didn't know existed, or small towns we have only driven by or maybe gone quickly through once or twice. The day may include stopping at a favorite ice cream shop for a certain flavor we prefer, or a new one we haven't tried. Our schedule is very flexible and open to any change that seems to want to happen.

During our rides we have taken some dead-end roads, driven by little quaint houses on unknown side streets, had conversations with people we have never met before but who greet us with smiles and follow up with good conversation about recent happenings in their worlds. All people have stories to tell. There are myriads of topics to discuss, but once thing we almost always talk about is "change," especially as we look back over several decades of having been sojourners of this beautiful-smooth-bumpy-confusing-incredible planet.

As I think about these times of exploration, I am aware of how much they metaphorically represent the out-picturing of change in our lives. We begin life in one place, not giving much thought to what lies ahead as we snuggle in and then adapt to the small world around us. Then one day we realize there is so much more to be investigated outside of our comfort zone. And so we expand our realm of experiences bit by bit until we see the whole world as one great playground of possibilities, and we venture forth even further.

As we set forth to discover what is out there in the unknown, alluring and beckoning world of life, we find that some roadways start off smooth, then get a little bumpy or even turn into dead ends. Other roads seem to flow smoothly and to be without end, yet much to our surprise we end up being faced with unforeseen circumstances that force us to turn around, pause, recalculate and head in another direction. Sometimes we have more than one direction available and we stand at the fork in the road wondering which one to take. Disappointment or confusion may set in. Or maybe joy, depending on the circumstances.

This can happen more than once in the span of our lifetime, no matter how much we prepare, stand our ground, think we know what we are doing, or actually move that mountain out of the way. We have given one simple word to this phenomenon: CHANGE. The experience of change, no matter how it is languaged, is experienced in every corner, culture, and personal life of people in the world. None of us are left untouched by change. Some change is brought about by necessity. Some comes unexpectedly and we fight it with all our strength, while describing it with highly energized four-letter words. There are also times when we are unexpectedly blessed with change. I celebrate those times, and I'm sure you do too.

Amusingly, as I have been typing this article over the last forty-five minutes, my whole schedule for the week has been changed by emails, phone calls and text messages. Only one thing is the same as it was this morning—really and literally. That's the truth. Guess I am getting my lesson in adapting to change. Ha ha!

I don't have all the answers as to what to do with "Change," except after doing my share of complaining at times, to just accept it, adapt as best I can, then move on to hopefully something even better. Here are a few quotes that have helped me along the way. Perhaps you will find one that speaks to you.

"One day your life will flash before your eyes. Make sure it is worth watching."

—Unknown

"By changing nothing, nothing changes."

—Tony Robbins

"We cannot discover new oceans unless we have the courage to lose sight of the shore."

—Andre Gide

"The greatest mistake you can make in life is to be constantly fearing you will make one."

—Elbert Hubbard

"If you run, you stand a chance of losing, but if you don't run, you have already lost."

—Barack Obama

"They say time changes things, but you actually have to change them yourself."

—Andy Warhol

"You are braver than you believe, stronger than you seem, and smarter than you think."

—A.A. Milne

"Life is a series of natural and spontaneous changes. To resist them is to bring sorrow. Let reality be reality. Let things flow naturally in whatever way they like."

—Lao Tzu

Accomplishing anything great in life requires significant change that sometimes pushes us beyond our comfort zone.

THE POWER OF
SELF-ESTEEM

I n scanning headlines of the newspaper this week—I rarely read beyond basic headlines anymore—some words jumped out at me as being thoughts that disempower us in so many ways because of their negativity. How can one be positive about much when, in bold print, we read—captured, killed, doubt, charges against, gunpoint, arrested, forced, attacked, despondent, lawsuit, shootings, implicated, terrorized, etc., and all within the first three pages. When I was a kid we used to shout at other kids when they teased us *Sticks and stones may break my bones, but words can never hurt me,* knowing full well that inside we were hurting because cruel words punctured holes in our self-esteem at a deep level.

The same is true for us in the adult world. We understand, at a deep level, even if we won't admit it, that words such as the ones mentioned above can impact us on a feeling level, even if not directed at us personally. These feelings erode our self-esteem because of that feeling of powerlessness to change the outer reality of our world. I have heard it said *I thought I could make a difference while I'm here, but I can't seem to do that.* And, then, we begin to feel less than, and sometimes give up moving into our full power and potential.

The Dalai Lama said, *If you see yourself in others, then whom can you harm?* The "self" we see in others has to be a healthy, confident, powerful and caring person in order for there to be no transfer of negative vision seen in others. Therefore, the words we read or use in our lives need to be those that lead us to allowing what we see in ourselves to be seen in others in a positive way. And, I know I am preaching to the choir, here.

WHO AM I TO BE?

T he first nine years of my life was spent in Portland, Oregon and thus, who I was at that time was defined by the provisions and expectations of living in a very large community. We did not have a car, so we either walked everywhere or took a combination of bus and streetcar. Grocery shopping was done by walking to the nearest small market or to the butcher shop for our supply of meat products. All the walking kept us all, old and young alike, quite physically fit. Life was simple when our activities kept us within the boundaries of our smaller neighborhood. It became much more complicated when we stepped outside of that comfort zone and were no longer defined my membership within that circle.

It was while walking to school that the confusion of identity proved a challenge. It was not because of the distance, about 8+ blocks as I recall, but because my neighborhood was known as the German-Polish section of the city, and it was the WWII era. My ethnic background was not very popular at that time. Therefore, who I was had multiple labels: my given name that identified me in relation to my family, church, and schoolmates, and the names I was called on the way to school by those who did not appreciate me or my family's presence in the community.

I was often bombarded with shouts of "krautkinder"

(English slang for young German child) in spite of my being a 3rd generation American and "Polska-baba" (Polish infant), not because I was Polish per se, but because I walked to school with a boy who was. Because of the slurs and often having things thrown at us (including pebbles) as we exited our closely-knit neighborhood and crossed over that invisible line into the not-so-ethnic area around our school, we were sometimes accompanied by adult family members. When we had our air raid drills at school, some people yelled at us as if the need for the raids was our fault. When all these things happened, I knew I didn't want to be who I was, but I also didn't know what else to be. I was too young to understand it all, but I knew I wanted to be free from it and just be a happier, more accepted me.

Being labeled has a way of making you wonder who you are and why you can't just be the person you know you are on the inside, and this makes the world a very confusing place. Obviously, I outgrew much of the stigma and found my place in the world, but while all is forgiven, it is not easily forgotten. How much better it would be, however, if these things are determined by the wisdom within ourselves and not by the expectations of others.

RIDING A CAMEL

⚘

I have ridden a camel three different times in my life, each time with different outcomes on a personal as well as physical level. As a young child, my legs didn't quite fit over the edges of the camel saddle very well and the height of the camel was a little daunting. Yet the camel's swaying motion was pleasant and relaxing, and since the camel was being led and my mom was close by, I quickly got over any fears.

The second time was during college. My main goal was to prove to myself and my friends that camel riding was not a big deal since I was "experienced" and could bump and sway along with the best of them...which I did, even when the camel decided to spit at the crowd and empty its bladder when we came to a stop. That happened at the end of the day, so the camel was probably tired of the weight on its back—a feeling I could relate to sometimes. Anyway, my friends were duly impressed and my ego was appreciative.

The third time, which occurred when I was in ministerial school at Unity Village, Missouri, was a very different experience. A friend and I decided to take a day off and go into Kansas City, with a stop at the zoo included in our itinerary. I was looking forward to seeing the animals, in spite of how I felt about their being locked up all the time and not in their natural habitat. I had not expected to see a camel there, much less one giving rides. This was Missouri and though the climate can be hot and the land is very flat, camels seemed really out of place when standing near the entrance gate. It seemed a bit strange that there was no line, but I was glad we didn't have to wait too long as it was a very warm day and we were ready for a break.

A gentleman with very dark eyes and smooth, darker skin was welcoming, but he seemed surprised that I was interested in a ride. Once seated on the camel, I ran my hand along its shoulder and spoke to it. My hand gradually became very warm and then almost hot. As I pulled it back the warmth spread through my whole body. I couldn't explain it, but wanted to believe the camel and I had just begun a conversation of some kind. I touched the saddle. Nothing. With my other hand I stroked the other shoulder. Same thing happened. As the camel turned its head slightly, I noticed its eyes were closed. I asked the man if this meant it was too tired to go on. "No," he replied in accented English. "He is meditating and preparing for your ride."

Throughout the ride I kept my eyes closed and pretended I was riding through the desert long, long ago, dressed in long robes—not fancy ones, but quality cloth and with a breeze moving the cloth that covered my head (like images from some movies and paintings I'd seen). I remember talking to Spirit and saying, "I'm not a man, but a woman. Yet, I am feeling something. What is it?" I received no reply of any note, but I felt really quiet inside. We thanked the camel, each of us, and left in silence, discussing the experience in the car as we drove away.

"Meditating and preparing for your ride," the man had said. A hump-backed camel, out of its element, carrying human bodies hour after hour, taking time to meditate? How often, in our lives do we feel out of our element, carrying a heavy load longer than planned and thinking there is no end in sight? I've been there—have you? How often have we forgotten to prepare ahead for those times so that we can, without becoming anxious or frustrated, keep moving forward until we arrive in another territory or another way of being in the world? Lesson from a camel: turn inward, listen, and prepare. For while the journey across the sands of time can seem endless, with faith we know there is an oasis of living, spiritual water waiting to nourish us in mind, body and soul. Whatever faith means to you, we all carry the same, essential, internal essence within us to help us through anything. "Lo, I am with you for always" is the ancient, ever-new promise.

Christmas is about the Light coming into the world. About the Faith of people who followed the Star of their inner knowing. About Acceptance of our oneness with the Universal Power which comes to us veiled or robed in the garments of love, offering to guide us across the desert of life and bless us each step of the way.

THE HOUSE OF BREAD

One year, just before Christmas, when I had a group of 5th graders around me on the rug where we circled up to do "class business," I asked them what their favorite Christmas song was. If I knew the words to what they mentioned, I would have us all sing the song—not all the verses, of course, but the main one. This was in the days when it was ok to sing Silent Night if it came up, but mostly kids songs were mentioned and always "Deck the Halls" and "Jingle Bells" and "Rudolph the Red-nosed Reindeer." I usually offered "I'll be home for Christmas," which they thought was too weird but they indulged me, even if I had to do it solo.

However, this one year we had a new boy in class and his choice was "On the Road Again." When I asked him why that song, he said, "Because we are always having to go to my mom's relatives house for something and take food that spills in the car, and then we have to travel a long way to see my dad's parents and I get so bored 'cause we have to wait to open presents." So we sang "On the Road Again" for Chris, though I forgot some of the words. They knew more than I did. Traveling at Christmas was big for this kid, as it was Mary and Joseph in the story told about that time over two thousand years ago. But the end result of their journey was truly a gift to be opened and it changed the world forever.

This memory brings to mind what Jon, Inge and I will be sharing this coming Sunday on "Three Travelers on the Road to Bethlehem." Jon has decided that two of the Magi were women for this occasion, which made me smile, and remember the words on a plaque in my hallway about three women who traveled to help the Holu Family on the evening of Jesus' birth. It reads like this and I hope it will bring a smile in the midst of your busy and hurried lives:

> The three women would have:
> Asked directions
> Arrived on time
> Cleaned the stable
> Made a casserole
> Helped deliver the baby
> Brought practical gifts
> And
> There would have been peace on earth

Bethlehem was the destination for Mary and Joseph, and it ours even today for being known as "the house of bread" and "the house of peace." We travel together in this life… to Bethlehem…to be with each other and to be fed and nourished both physically and spiritually and to be uplifted in conscious oneness with "the One." We work together to bring peace to the world because we care enough to want to bring and set our souls' gifts at the feet of all people everywhere. We are the Christ in expression.

On a bit of a side note here, however, Bethlehem bears the modern name of Beit-Lahm, which means "house of flesh." Perhaps our prayers of conscious intention need to be ones of holding all the world in our hearts and of lifting up the consciousness everywhere so that peace on earth can become a reality in our time. I think God could use a helping hand right now.

THE GIFTS OF OUR
NATURAL PASSION

―――⚬⚬⚬――――

O ne of my passions has always been reading biographies and autobiographies of people who lived with passion and made a difference in the world. It started way back when I was in 6th grade and read an autobiography of Pearl Buck, author of "The Good Earth". I responded to her thoughts and words because writing was her passion, and it was also mine. Through the years I have continued daily to look for more words of wisdom from people who have lived their passion and I've always found something to carry me through all the ups and downs of life. I share a tiny bit of this with you now.

Howard Thurman, influential African American author, philosopher, theologian, educator and founder of one of the first multicultural churches in 1944, wrote: "Don't worry about what the world needs. Ask what makes you come alive and do that, because what the world needs is people who have come alive."

So I ask you, "What makes you come alive?" Maybe, like me, it's more than one thing and maybe different things at different times, depending on what you have newly discovered that you did not know existed or was possible. If you look closely, however, there remains a common thread of passion that began before you even knew you had a life to put together. It was your gift at birth. You may have noticed how it follows you around and sits on your soul.

"Finding your passion is like finding your personal roadmap. When you know what your passion is, you feel motivated, inspired, and so much clearer about what your next step should be." (Ashley Wilhite—founder of Your Super Awesome Life). She suggests 8 things to discover that personal passion—at any age: 1) Slow down and listen to yourself, 2) Change your story to one of confidence and courage, 3) Own and celebrate your uniqueness, 4) Believe in yourself, 5) Find themes—what are you drawn to again and again because it brings you joy and light, 6) Write and write and process your thoughts without influence from the outside world, 7) Focus on fun—what makes you smile and do that, 8) Push past your fear—over time you will find yourself being steered toward an authentic, purposeful and passionate life that might have been blocked in the past because fear held you back.

Being passionate about life does not mean you will always be laughing, smiling and not have challenges. Your passion is there to give you refuge, something to wrap you in serenity, to bless you with knowing all is ok. In that knowing challenges can be met and overcome. I don't walk around all day high on passionate ecstasy, but there is a calm center that cannot be disturbed because I know I am where I am supposed to be. It took me a while to get here, but it is a good place. May you find what brings you joy, act on it, nourish it, practice it, share it and feel your heart smiling more each day. The bonus is that when you do, you bless others as well.

TWO ROADS WELL TRAVELED

Part of my growing up years was spent on our strawberry farm in rural Yamhill County and since this was the time before mass paving of roads, my sister and I got to know gravel roads pretty well as we walked them to our elementary school and then to catch the bus to high school, which was three miles away. Because we were 8 years apart in age, we trekked them separately. We have discussed our impressions and experiences often in recent years and share great stories and surprisingly so, some similar impressions.

The first road was reached by taking a short path north, and down the hill, to the gravel road that eventually crossed a quiet highway and led us to our two room elementary schoolhouse. Grades 1-8. This walk was about ¾ of a mile long. It meant a slippery hillside when it rained, sitting on our bottoms to slide down the hill when the rain turned to ice, or getting our saddle shoes filled with dusty dirt in dry weather. When we finally got bikes in about 6th grade, we had to push them up the hill. We called this walk our "self-sufficiency training". Our mother told us later how she would go to the crest of the hill and check on us, but she knew we needed to know how to navigate in the physical world. (Remember, we were alone, not together)

The second road led in the southerly direction from our driveway, down the other side of the hill and was gravel all the way to the highway where we caught the high school bus. This road was only about a half mile long and we passed only two houses. On rainy days we could huddle in a small wooden structure by the bus stop to avoid getting too wet. We both remember the smell of rain on the oak trees, the strong winds that blew over this part of the hill from the west, messing up our hair, sitting in the tall grasses by the side of the road to rest, the gnarly apples from deformed, ancient apple trees, our walking slowly if we did not want to face farm chores, and Mr. Davies who said we were the smartest girls in the world –at each of our individual time of trekking.

The second walk we called our " voyage out into the world". Two different roads, two different growing experiences, different careers for my sister and I, two lives now in their so called "golden years". And yet, the memories of those days "on the road" so to speak, hold more memories than any other in our lives. I believe it is because we were traveling to ourselves, to who we were and still are, in spite of all that has taken place since.

I have a belief that there is no road that is less traveled than any other when it comes to the road that leads "home." I'm on the road again.

A HIDING PLACE

———✷———

B efore I turned 12 and other things began to take up my time, there was usually a couple of spaces of time during the week, between chores, homework and babysitting for the neighbors, when I would be able to wander off to my special place in the wooded area just beyond our house and across my father's strawberry patch, where I had my created my own special get-away world. It consisted of a pile of rocks my father let me have, leftover from the gravel he used in our dirt-bed driveway. In my imagination this was a sandy beach. On one side of the rock pile there was a tree stump about 4 feet high, which I draped with strips of cloth. It became my waterfall. As a result, I could live in my pretend world that I called "My Hawaii Beach Place." Sometimes it was my "Polynesian Place." I had never been to either of them, but read about it in National Geographic and my geography book from school. But I knew they were special and so I created them for myself.

Around the circle of rocks I set various stuffed, rubber made, and wooden oak tree limb "animals" and would tell stories to them, or sometimes read stories. I imagined they talked back to me. This world worked well in Spring, Summer and Fall, but got pretty shabby in the winter when I had to take the animals inside. Sometimes we would go—

animals in a big bucket—during snow times—but we didn't stay long. Just checked the place out.

The remembrance of this came back to me this last week when I read the title of Jon's talk that was coming up: "The Shared Message of the Greatest Souls in History." What if we created a large sandy "beach" in our imaginations and brought to that circle some of the great souls "from the ages," had them join the circle and then let them speak to us? What might they say? I'm sharing a few my favorites with you. I had to leave so many of them out, but I know you all have many of your own. (You may not recognize many of these people, but they are still great souls in their own right.

"There are many paths to enlightenment. Be sure to take the one with a heart."

—Lao-tzu

"If you are enlightened, you are not free—you are freedom itself. Not like a bird in the sky, but the bird itself."

—William Keers

"A person who says "I am enlightened, probably isn't…"

—Ram Dass

"Laughter is the shortest distance between two people."

—Victor Borge

"The more we forget ourselves in giving to others, the better we can understand what love really is."

—J. Donald Walters

"Love doesn't make the world go round. Love is what makes the ride worthwhile."

—F.P. Jones

"I am realizing every day that the search for truth is in vain unless it is founded upon love."

—Mohandas Gandhi

"Love is a fruit in season at all times and within the reach of every hand."

—Mother Teresa

"You are part of the universe, no less than the stars and trees, and you have a right to be here. And whether it is clear to you or not, the universe is unfolding as it should."

—Desiderata

"For every minute you are angry, you lose 60 seconds of happiness."

—Ralph Waldo Emerson

"Blessed is the person who can enjoy the small things, the common beauties, the day-by-day events, sunshine on the fields, birds on the bough, breakfast, dinner, supper, a friend passing by. SO many people who go afar for enjoyment, will find they have left it behind at home."

—David Grayson

"It isn't more light we need, it's putting into practice what light we already have."

—Peace Pilgrim

"The world is full of so many things. I'm sure we all should be happy as kings."

—Robert Louis Stevenson.

Again, not all of these people quoted here may seem to be of the greatest souls in history. However, the wisdom spoken qualifies them for inclusion in that category, as far as I am concerned. And there is one more—the stuffed tiger that I had in my place in the woods who spoke to me these words: " Know that you are worthy of the blessings that come your way.". It was written on the tag around its neck, by the friend that gave it to me. I still have the tag, but "Tilly Tiger" has been gone for quite a number of years, having been loved by so many children in my classrooms.

IN MY NEXT LIFE

A few days ago, while observing appropriate social distancing, a good friend of mine and I enjoyed delicious Hawaiian lunches seated on a bench in one of the most beautiful, expansive and user friendly parks in the area. The sun was bright, the temperature perfect, the shade not too cool and the light breeze kept us from feeling the reported temperature at that time of 82 degrees. It was a perfect park day in all ways and those who either walked, ran, rode bikes or skate boarded through the area seemed to agree. Smiles and friendly nods were abundant. Except for our masks, which we obviously had to remove for eating, and hand sanitizer, it felt like quite a normal day.

During our time there the ducks and geese that have made the park area their seemingly year-round home, since we have seen them there year round, came single filing up from the river and seemed interested in whether or not we might have some leftovers to share. They seemed to not be aware of the sign that says we are not to accommodate them. We wondered what they think about all that is going on right now or if they even cared since it does not seem to have interrupted their routine. We also talked and wondered what it must be like to be a feathered being, if maybe we had been one in another life, or if we might become one in the next since some philosophies say we go through all kinds of incarnations. What would we like to be if that became available to us next time around? We both agreed we might have been cats at one time, but never settled on what each of us might like to be for our next choice, if we get a choice that is. We just knew we wanted to serve a purpose and to be peaceful beings.

After I got home I emailed a young friend of mine and asked him the question, "Kenny, when you come back in the next life, what do you want to be?" I know he believes in the coming back philosophy. It's his unusual and unexpected response that I want to share with you. "I want to come back as a virus." He said. "What? Are you kidding?" I responded. "Whatever for?" He responded that, as we are finding out, a virus can travel far and wide in a short amount of time and affect millions of people, which results in great changes in the world. He said he would come back as a "Love Virus". It would be one that, though had some prickly points so as to easily attach to the human heart, it would also be colorful and if one listened closely, one could hear the belly laugh inside of it that comes from the joy of spreading the good news of healing, wholeness, joy, love, caring, compassion and all the other things that support the unfolding of the human body and soul.

I cannot deny, or argue with, the beauty of that perspective. And, I can see that, even though that is not the intent of this mindless, invasive, prickly-looking virus that is with us now, we –as people who are resilient, creative, determined, life-affirming beings, began quite beautifully responding in ways that we never expected. Friends contacting friends, families learning to get along better, beautiful poetry, music, abundant flower gardens being planted, renewed interest in food gardens, creative food prep, assisting others to feel loved and acknowledged through virtual presentations, etc., etc., and returned, as one of my life-long friends said, to the better times in history.

My desire, of course, is that, we be released soon from being the unwitting host of that prickly looking thing we see pictures of, so we can return to some normalcy—including being physically present with each other again, to touch and hug and exchange flesh and blood smiles with each other and see the sparkles in each other's eyes, and share meals, trips and other good things. But, I also hope we will bring the good things we have learned from this along with us and never let them go again. Never. Never.

Being in the park with a friend, sharing a meal, talking with the feathered ones, seeing the sun on the water and feeling the breeze on one's face = paradise. Whether in human or animal form, if my next life has only this, I would be the happiest of souls. What would you like to experience?

OBSERVATIONS

W hen I was a child, I often felt as if I was really just an observer of the world around me, and not an integral part of much of it. I would watch people as they busied themselves with activities, and then watch the activities unfold — like it was all a movie on a screen. I would even go so far as to evaluate which of the scenes I was viewing would I keep as is and which ones would I change if it were me creating them. It seemed like while this reality was playing out, there was another reality somewhere that I could not touch, or see, but it was hovering around somewhere. I wondered if I was the only one, or were there others—either children or adults—who felt the same way.

This internally focused realm caused one of my 8th grade teachers to express concern to my parents that I was possibly too much of an introvert and maybe they should look at that. I overheard my mother telling a neighbor about that one day over coffee when they assumed I was out doing my farm chores. As they say, that "rattled my cage." Me an introvert? I had to look up the word in the giant dictionary that sat on an end table in our living room. What I read shocked me. That's not me, I thought; but I did contemplate that a lot for the next few months. I had friends I did things with, family who seemed to think I was ok, even when I headed for my favorite apple tree in our big orchard with a good book.

It wasn't until the next year when I went to high school, that I realized that whatever was inside me obviously needed to come out and it was thanks to a special teacher that I began to "burst forth on the scene" in entirely new ways. Dance classes, choir, high school plays, member of student council, editor of the school newspaper and eventually queen of the "Cotton Ball"—an event as big as the prom—and two guys to take me to the prom. This continued through college. I think I must have been pretty obnoxious at times, along with it all.

The point: Deepak Chopra says this: "The soul is on a journey through cosmic time and you can orchestrate your journey through cosmic time when you have awakened to the bigger reality." Maybe, for some people, the bigger reality is the first level of awareness through which they come and then have to learn to do earth school. I'm not saying I came here enlightened, or anything like that at all, please hear that. It just took me a while—a whole 10 years, to adjust to being on the planet. And, truth be told, I am truly still working on that. That alone has given me a rich and full life, and that richness and fullness continue to bless me, even when I fall flat on my face, which can be quite often.

Relying on a wonderful, merciful, loving, compassionate, graceful and Divine Spirit is required at all times as we take this journey. C.S. Lewis wrote: "Relying on God has to begin all over again each day, as if nothing had yet been done. From this we get our strength to carry on." If we begin each day invoking Spirit's presence, either through meditation, prayer, or just a thank you shout to the sun, our soul's journey through cosmic time can be a grand adventure.

Appreciating

———⬤⬤⬤———

"Appreciation is the highest form of prayer for it acknowledges the presence of good wherever you shine the light of your thankful thoughts."

—Alan Cohen

ON HOLY COMMON GROUND

I'm in awe—I always am during this time of year when the trees bloom in all their splendor—bursting forth in reds, golds, yellows, browns, and various fading shades of green. To me, Spring blossoms are portents of things to come in the fall when trees, which have prepared for the golden fulfillment of their purpose, release their hidden splendor in a most magnificent array of color. Standing as stalwart supporters of this magnificence are the evergreens, keeping the verdant hues that serve as a perfect backdrop for the show this tree kingdom is providing as it leads us into our seasonal time of rest and renewal.

As the drive I was participating in on a sunny Sunday afternoon expanded into more miles than anticipated, there was a point at which I felt so grateful for everything I was seeing and experiencing, that my eyes got misty, and the words to a favorite song came to mind. It was written in 1983 by Geron Davis and sung by various artists through the years. Each time I hear it I am humbled, even though some of the words are not ones I use these days to express the Divine Presence; but, that doesn't matter because the power of the melody and the message is timeless and profound. Here is a little bit of the lyrics: (I have done a bit of tweaking to help it match the out of doors instead of the indoors indicated in the main lyrics.)

"...*Oh, we are standing on Holy Ground and I know, I know there are angels all around. Let us praise Him (Her) now, for we are standing in {The Presence} on Holy Ground. There is joy beyond all measure and...sweet peace of mind can be found...reach out and claim it, for we are standing on Holy Ground.*"

With those words came the thought of "common ground". If the evergreens can share common grounds with the leaved ones, certainly we, as people of the earth on which they live, can, perhaps by watching and learning from them, figure out how to find enough common ground to be able to come together in the spirit of Love and Caring and find solutions to all that is calling forth to be healed on this planet. It has been said by many: "*The left wing and the right wing belong to the same bird.*" How do we learn to understand this truth to the point that we can, in our diversity, stand as one—while working together individually and collectively while accepting each of our special gifts, talents and wisdoms—create a display of wondrous beauty, build a place of peace, and then together release splendor beyond anything ever known for all the universe to see? A few thought on this:

- We have to choose common ground. Find what we have in common, then choose which one we want to be a part of and work on, because we can't all do it all.

- Be ready to face hardships, hurts, ridicule and judgement. That's what it takes sometimes to secure human freedom, but it is in that freedom that we find our true common ground because it is what our hearts and souls long for.

- Division doesn't fit our world view of what we want. That has become very evident. What we want is that "town square" where we can come together in our diversity and share who we are, what we are, how we feel and be accepted. To do that we have to choose Love. We can't lead if we don't Love. We can't find common ground, or even Holy ground, if there is not Love.

- Love those who might not love us back.

- Accept uncomfortableness for a while and step into our courage. Be bigger, stronger, bolder, even if just in our own space, our homes, our community.

- It's easy to find commonality in our love for babies, or our dogs and cats, or our favorite ice cream. But what we love goes deeper than that. Find it, find others who share in that, and invite in those who aren't sure we want them in our love circle and then love them, until who they are shines brighter than the brightest star.

- We share the internet—but are we an inter-net within our communities that invites others in?

- For people of faith it all involves a belief in a Higher Power, and a level of humility to know we are dependent on that Higher Power. That power has chosen to live within us and is available at all times.

In the forests, the parks, and by our rivers, a seed is dropped, a tree grows—the community of trees, in all their diversity make room for that seedling to grow to whatever height or kind or color it was meant to be. It pays us back by either staying verdantly green, or showing us the splendor of its mature autumn colors. It does this on Holy Ground…and mixed company. We can do the same on our Holy Common Ground when we find it. What splendor will be created when we do.

We are to have some rain for a few days, but now I am committed to two walks a day outside, though the ground may be a little slippery at times and I will need a warm coat, I will return to the trees and let them teach me. I have more lessons to learn. Don't we all.

In the expansive Love that comes from
a wonderful Sunday drive,

Sherry

BEYOND THE SHADOW
OF A DUCK

I've been spending a lot of time in parks these days, both for exercise and fresh air, with the added bonus of the stress release that comes from being in the presence of other people. Whether they are just walking or running by and keeping distance, yet smiling, or whether it is with a friend seated the proper distance away on a park bench, sharing lunchtime or just talking. I'm finding that being in the house too much was just not working for me, so this has become part of my daily routine and what a blessing that has been. I read reports from some of you that get to go to the coast, mountains and other places with a bit of envy, as I have not driven long distances for a few years. I am practicing though, in small little steps and hope to get there soon.

At certain times of day in my favorite park, the ducks come away from the coolness of the river and take a walk up to where people are, stand very close at times, and wait to be both acknowledged and hopefully fed some morsel from a lunch or a pocket. They are so special to me and seem so very accepting of their world as it is. I honor their independence and yet their collectiveness in that they have all those others of their kind around them much of the time. It says something, to me at least, about community and how all creatures great and small do better when they have contact with each other.

One thing I have noticed in particular is that, no matter when small or large gatherings of ducks happen, standing apart from the group, but not too much, is one larger duck, usually in the shadows, surveying the group. On occasion, this one duck will waddle over to one of the others and "say" something, or sort of nudge them along and eventually will lead them or the group to their next place. I call this one "The God Duck". The one who lets the others roam at will, until the time comes when it is best for them to do the next thing. Sometimes one duck is a little slow in getting into action and the God Duck will actually nudge it with its beak.

As this God Duck stands in the shadow, somewhere behind the shadow of this duck, unseen but not unknown to them is, I believe, an intelligence that provides a knowing, a wisdom, and yes, an intelligence to make decisions based on the needs of the group. Divine Timing, in duck-mind and then in duck-land. Scientist call it radar—I call it Divine Mind.

And so it is with us. We plan, carry out our plans and then begin planning the next thing—or not. No matter where we are, what we are doing, even when we are not sure about the next steps, if we stop for a moment and listen to the inner voice, we can become like the flock of the God Duck—guided in the right direction at the right time. When we get this sequence in alignment, we can then have ourselves in the place of helpfulness when called upon to be the God Duck for others. It's when we veer off from that place and take too many things in our own hands and try to make them happen, that we meet with challenges that throw us off center, at which point we are not very helpful to ourselves, or to others.

Our being here at all, in this life, this body, this place in time—tough as it is—is so very special because we are asked now, more than ever before, to be present for each other. I so miss the physical presence of my "people" and my flock seems scattered, as do my thoughts and feelings. So I go to the park, seek out the God Duck, watch his flock be guided, and pray for the day when we can all be together again in close community. In the meantime that Divine Spirit that sometimes seems to be hidden in the shadows, offers to step in and guide us, like the duck flock, to the cool and refreshing waters of the river of life.

I am still learning about that which is beyond the shadow of a duck, and giving thanks for our feathered friends, and all the creatures great and small.

Love,

Sherry

SOMEWHERE IN TIME

I t began in this way:

> "Dear Sherry, My name is Janet Powell and I live
> in England in a place called Chelmsford. It is in
> Essex County. I am 9 years old. We have just had
> a terrible war, but because it is over now I want to
> have a pen friend in the United States. I saw your
> name in the newspaper saying you would like a pen
> friend, too. I am wondering if you would like to be
> my pen friend? I am hoping you will. My mum says
> it would be nice if we could do that. Please let me
> know soon. With hope, Janet."

And so, in 1945, between the time that WWII ended in
Europe in May, and the final signing of the official surrender
by the Japanese government in September, a friendship was
born between two young girls who lived a half a globe apart.
It was a friendship that lasted for seventy four years—Janet
passed away in the fall of 2019. It was a friendship filled
with sharings of usual girl things of that era—clothes, family
activities, trips, photographs, girlhood romances, and eventually courtships, marriages, and children. It was a time also
when I was able to send her some things that were in very low
supply in Europe due to the effects of the war, and in return,

she sent me small gifts, some of which she made, and which I still have. When Queen Elizabeth ascended the throne, following the death of her father, I received coronation books, postcards and other memorabilia, which I also saved.

Janet and her husband, Joe Russell had two children—a daughter named Lesley and a son named Greg. They came as a family to visit my family here in Oregon twice and my daughter and I visited them in England for a month, where we were joined by my husband Bob on his way back from Egypt. We agreed to meet again in England, but it was not to be. I feel sad about that at times; but in spite of failed plans it was a friendship that was always very real, very tangible and heart-felt and I can still hear her voice, see her smile and feel the love that grew over the years between the two of us, and our families as well. I hear from her daughter in various ways and look forward to a visit when COVID decides to let go of the world.

So why this story? Because the time to rummage through memory boxes, look at old photographs, and read letters received through the years, has been part of my therapy during these times that have bewildered, saddened, confused and humbled me. This is one of the many gifts that more time alone, out of the busyness of "the other routine," has opened for me. I know that many of you have found the gifts also these days and I would love to hear your stories. Some of you have shared them with me and in that sharing we, too, have become new friends again, and closer in spirit, and hope, and vision for our lives.

Emily Dickinson said: "Hope is the thing with feathers that perches in the soul—and sings the tunes without the words and never stops at all." As I spend quality time with special friends, whether virtually, in person, by email, or letter—whatever—I hear the ongoing tune and that carries me forward, sometimes with tears, sometimes with laughter, sometimes with another set of even bigger questions, but the melody blesses my soul and gives me hope that we can be the change we want to see in the world.

Somewhere in time there will come that conscious awareness that the way we, as a global family, truly and deeply want to show up in the world, can happen when we build friendships and join with others in keeping the dream, and the hope, alive.

I remember when the cost of sending an airmail letter to Janet rose to 58 cents and I had to pick a few more strawberries or beans to make the extra money—or iron a few more clothes for our neighbor for whom I worked after school. I also remember the joy of being taken to the small rural post office near my home so I could buy that stamp, lick it and make sure it stuck to the somewhat slippery paper. Then, after an amount of time, checking the mailbox at the end of our driveway every day to see if she had written back. The exchange of letters was one of the highlights of my growing up. Today I still treasure paper letters and cards when they appear in my mailbox and I save them all. Some special ones sit in a small metal rack on my office desk and I look at them quite often. Somewhere in time, a connection was made that lasts forever and I treasure that.

What is on your heart at this time? (As you can tell, special friendships are on mine). If I could tie this in to some spiritual teaching—which is not as easy as I thought, it would be (maybe because of the emotion that rises up in me)—perhaps, the second commandment Jesus left with us, "Love your neighbor as yourself." Yes. I like that. Enough said.

Your friend,

Sherry

THE SIDEWALK SWEEPER, THE FRENCH MAIDEN AND THE UNKNOWN ELF

Kindnesses in the midst of Covid

I want to begin this essay with you by sharing a song. One that came to mind after I witnessed a very special ritual while attending my Sunday in the Park church service one day. Many of you will be able to hum along as you remember the tune to that special song about the old time lamplighter that is often sung around the time of the Christmas season. This is my summer time version:

"He makes the daytime so much brighter, wherever he does go.

The kindly sidewalk sweeper, that I've come to know.

The laughing children share their chatter, knowing what is so

In the heart of the sidewalk sweeper, that we both have come to know."

The sidewalk sweeper gives loving service by sweeping and tidying up in various areas where the public might be walking or the playground where children and their families are playing together while enjoying their time in the park. He has also blessed our church by clearing the walks and the fallen stuff around plants and taking the debris that has fallen from the trees over to the dumpster. This tidying up, which has not gone unnoticed by observers, makes a real difference not only in the general appearance of things, but he shares these unconditional acts from a place of honoring and joy. I hope he knows how much he is admired and appreciated.

One day a week, a lovely young woman with a beautiful French name receives my list of groceries and other needs and goes shopping for me. She is so gentle and loving in her acceptance of my limitations due to the virus and says she enjoys doing this. We have become good friends and my life is blest—again. It is her way of giving back to the world at this time and I am blest. She does other volunteer acts of kindness to fill the time after losing her job in a bakery when they had to cut back on staff. I think of her as a beautiful expression of the heart of many young people today that may never get recognition for their generosity.

Yesterday morning there appeared, once again, on my doorstep, a small box of chocolates. This was, I think, about surprise number fifteen over the past few months—something left in the same spot. Sometimes it is a small unopened box of cookies, or a small bouquet of flowers, or a note wishing me a happy day and please stay well and safe. I have no idea who this is so I just call that person the "Unknown Elf—or Elfette". I wonder to myself who would do this kind of thing and choose to remain anonymous and leaving me wondering how to thank them? So, I left a thank you note in the gift place the other day hoping it would open the door to knowing. All I got back was a piece of paper with a smiley face sticker on it. But that said so much to me and it let me know that communication had happened. I so hope they know the light these little things have brought into my life. If it is you, dear reader, know now how much your mystery adds to my days.

Sometimes I wonder about what all of "this" is about—I think you know what I mean by "this"—and will some of this goodness continue after things unfold in the hopefully better days to come. I believe it will, because I believe in the Goodness of people and that Love will win out. I believe that finding joy in the simple things has become more a way of life than it has for a long time. We are in a huge learning curve right now and, though this experience is not my preferred kind of scenario for unfoldment of the best in human nature and the world in general, it has brought about a space of time that allows us to consider what we value most in life and the time to act upon it.

Like you who have shared your struggles with me, I have gone through a lot of soul searching, anger, depression, tears, frustration etc., but I have also seen, experienced and heard about some amazing things that people have done to cope with their topsy-turvy lives. I think of the wonderful sweeper who, with his small broom and other tools, pushes aside the muck and clutter and makes places more beautiful and inviting and fresh for so many unknown to him. I think of my darling French maiden who, in all her young beauty chooses to put others first, and then the "Elf-Elfette" who takes time to think up surprises for bringing a smile and I know—beyond a shadow of a doubt—that there are angels in people's clothing doing their best to bring smiles, hope—anything of upliftment—to the people of this time.

There is a saying that a special friend of mine shares with me every once in a while. It is this: "A stranger is a friend I haven't met yet." Out there among all of you are so many good friends, and there are readers I haven't met yet. Thank you all for your kindnesses, wherever you work your magic. We are already friends and will perhaps meet some day. How nice is that?

> "They make the day a little brighter,
> wherever they may go,
> The kind and special people that we have
> come to know…And have yet to know."

In Love and Gratitude,

Sherry

THE GREATEST GIFT
IN LIFE

They stand in the driveway—the mother and the father—watching their son attempt to climb to the top of the jungle gym apparatus his father built for him. The little one is perhaps 3-4 years of age, his legs not very long, his attempts not very agile, but definitely showing determination to get as high as possible. The mother and the father issue forth words of encouragement, love and caring clearly in their voices. The little one stumbles and in trying to recover, falls to the ground and dissolves in tears.

The father races to his side, with the mother close behind—both uttering words of compassion, but also assuring him, with hugs and Kleenex tissues at work, that things like this can happen, but that he has everything he needs to make it to the top someday, and they will be there to help him do that whenever they can. They ask if he wants to try again, but amid sniffles, he says he didn't want to do that. "Then how about some ice cream?" the mother asks. The young boy shakes his head in agreement. The three walk toward the house hand in hand as the father says to his son, "You are really amazing. You know that?"

Watching this happen, while standing in my carport, I reached for one of my own tissues and wiped some smudged mascara off my face. In past times I have heard parents handle this differently with admonitions, harsh words and warnings, probably coming from fear. Sometimes parents use these things, not because they don't care, but to try to change behavior. The parents I witnessed used a different tactic that I know worked, because a few days later I saw them outside again, standing closer to the climbing structure and watching their son navigate upward once again and they again cheered him on.

I was sharing this approach to managing children with a good friend of mine as I expressed a wondering about how children today are doing with everything around the present pandemic — the more consistent confinement of the family within close quarters, no school, parents perhaps expressing worries and concerns, and a world that I'm sure is visibly different for the children the same as everyone else. In return, my friend shared these words from an email he recently sent to his children. I am inspired to share them with you because we all need to hear them, but most importantly, our children need these kinds of words as often as possible: "My Dad gave me the greatest gift in life…he believed in me! Yes, I have always believed in you both. You are more important to me than anything. So many wonderful memories of our times together…Happy Easter! Love always, Dad."

What we are facing now has turned our world upside down and it may never right itself in ways we expect, or desire, and we may have to climb a jungle-gym of our own to get on top of living, navigating, functioning and keeping hope alive in the new era we face. We may need to "parent" each other along the way. The saying that "we are in this together" is the bottom-line truth. What better way to be there for each other, and for our dear children who will be taking over as we age out of lives—though hopefully not too soon—than to tell each other "I believe in you. I believe you can do this. You are very important to me. I have fond memories of things we have shared and done together. I would not want to travel this road without you.

This is my truth for all of you. This is my gratitude for all I have been privileged to share with you, and my hope for more to come in the days ahead as we create a new paradigm for being "together" in the world. Let's model for our children, grandchildren, and all youth, the expression of our belief in them. Let's continue to appreciate our families, even when we are too close together for too long, and cherish and bless those who are lonely. Let's share our belief in them with them whenever we can. Let's also give thanks for what we are learning during these times. It's a hard lesson all around, but we can take the high road through it and come out the better for it.

Thank you my good friend, for sharing this with me, and subsequently with each one who reads this article. I am touched, honored and inspired.

COLORS OF THE
AUTUMN WIND

Took time today to stop on the side of a street with no traffic, small cozy houses, and dozens of beautiful trees in the process of releasing their blossoms onto the street in layers of incredibly beautiful colors. A brief moment in time away from phone calls, emails and text messages, even though I was on my way to church for a class, where I would re-enter that milieu of constant communication and decision making. Don't misunderstand, I love being at church and with my spiritual family—all are such an integral part of my life. But in this moment, immersed in the wonder of nature, the artist's colorful palette of promise and wonder, it seemed like the whole of the earth was the most important and captivating thing one should be contemplating.

Woven into the contemplation were these thoughts:

1. Why, with all this natural beauty around us, do we have to construct 5 story business buildings in quiet neighborhoods that block the view of the hillsides? Wouldn't a maximum of two stories be enough, if we have to build them here at all? Some visions are very limiting and only serve to squeeze

us into narrower lanes of mobility and keep our eyes on the ground instead of the sky. My personal soap box—forgive me.

2. Except for the cleaning of drains and gutters, why do we have to gather up all these beauties into piles that sit on the side of the street for months and decay into slippery messes until rescued eventually by debris trucks, long after parked cars have once again squished them down. Why not just let them scatter their loveliness on lawns and flutter across the streets for all to enjoy for a while. When I was growing up on the farm we never raked our leaves, except for some mulch piles in the orchard, or compost in the garden, as the leaves fed the lawns which turned a beautiful rich green in the Spring. I know—yes—my gutters need cleaning out too), but the frantic raking feels like we are afraid of the leaves, that they will pollute us somehow, which they can when we burn them in backyards. Soap box number 2.

3. They are taking some of our most beautiful trees and planting them on space stations to replicate planet earth's natural beauty because it feeds the soul of those who work there. From there maybe the rest of the planets in our galaxy can be beautified as well as grow produce to feed whatever or whoever. This just blows my mind, as they say, but it is a fact. Must have it pretty good here if it is worthy of replication. I want to treasure it even more.

4. The silence on the street was so profound for a
    few minutes and it was as if the air and the wind
    had drawn open a curtain, allowing the song of
    the earth and the breath of cosmic wholeness
    waft through, releasing all tensions. It all seemed
    so clear. Nothing was fuzzy anymore concerning
    our role in it all or what the universe is asking of
    us. Dare I—and we—step into the vastness of the
    cosmic consciousness available to us and allow
    ourselves to evolve into what we are meant to
    be. I think the earth itself would rejoice if we just
    accepted and for a moment I could see each leaf
    nodding in agreement.

5. Then a small child, probably about 6 or 7 came
    around the corner, hand in hand with his father,
    and holding up a painting of some kind. He was
    so excited about his art work that he withdrew his
    hand from his father's and pointed to something
    on the picture and energetically told more of the
    story. Sort of like "God-Spirit" saying "look—here
    –look at this—this is you, right here—this is what
    you, too, can do. Right here, right now. Will you
    accept? The father took the picture and looked at
    it more closely, said something that made the child
    smile, held it up against his heart and then up
    against the child's heart, beating under the colorful,
    apparently hand-made, light-weight sweater.

So here we are, immersed in the wonder of it all, focusing
on the next step, putting one foot in front of the other and,
as I have heard so much these days, walking just one step

at a time, because any other way is just too overwhelming. May we remember though, that each step is important, and nothing is more important at this time to do than that which needs to be done by us. May we keep the curtains of time and space open so we can peek through frequently, see the bigger picture of unlimited space and continue to build a future in which the consciousness of each person on earth is lifted up so high that only joy, acceptance, forgiveness, oneness and peace—all the "good things"- will fill the days of our lives and the space expanding out before us at this time in the unfolding of the cosmos. May we all breathe in beauty and, may our footsteps be light upon the earth while our eyes are on the " heavens," (consciousness expanded) for this holds all the promises of the future, if we will allow it.

I hope you will all find the parks, the rivers, the hills to hike, the breath of country air and other inspirational places to find your story of inspiration. I just had a brief time to engage, but it was truly amazing anyway.

THE EXPERIENCE
OF AWE

It happened one afternoon, right here in Eugene, in a building, on a hardwood floor, behind a row of movable cushioned chairs during the intermission of a special musical performance. Earlier, I had participated in a church service, had a delicious lunch in a nearby restaurant and happily settled myself into my assigned seat feeling quite awake and ready to absorb a performance I had been looking forward to very much. Even though the first half of the program was beautifully and inspirationally presented, by the end of the first act I found myself yawning and feeling a bit wilted. So as the intermission began, I uttered a simple little prayer asking for an infusion of energy and light. With full faith in the power of Spirit to answer my prayer, I sat quietly for a minute or so, but nothing happened.

Of course, I wondered why my usual approach didn't work as it so often did. I decided the next best thing would be to get up and walk, which I did. Seeing a friend of mine visiting with a small group, I moved in their direction. Seeing me approach, the people smiled and said hello. Then the miracle of awe happened. A young woman in the group with the brightest eyes and the most happily genuine smile one could imagine put her arms around my neck, told me she thought I was pretty and she loved me. She was quite a bit shorter than me and I had to bend over a bit. I would have gotten down on my knees for her if necessary. Not because she said those words, but because the energy coming from her made my body tingle. Spirit had answered my prayer through the open heart of a young woman with Down Syndrome. I will never forget that infusion of energy and the pureness and honesty on her face.

"God" does deliver—just not always through expected means. To me, that is what *awe* is all about: the unexpected, almost breathless experience of wonder and amazement that is something we could not have planned for in our human way. Awe can be defined in two ways: "An overwhelming feeling of wonder or admiration" and "profound respect for someone of something." Originally, in Middle English, it was defined as fearful or causing intense fear—from which we get the word "awful." Thank goodness it has evolved into its present form, which is often used as a synonym for "excellent."

An unknown author wrote: *"Each of us is the protagonist in our own life. Our aims and goals feel like the most important things in the world. However, for most of us, time feels scarce and as a result, accomplishing everything we want to can feel unattainable."* A related limiting belief is thinking or feeling we are insignificant, like one grain of sand on an enormous beach, while feeling the pressure to somehow be the whole beach. A sense of awe can challenge these limiting, seemingly hopeless beliefs. The truth is that we don't have to be the whole beach. There are other grains of sand creating the beach with us. Opening our eyes to this wondrous truth removes the pressure of thinking we are the most important person in the universe. As we allow others to co-create and co-sustain the shared beaches of our lives, we can relax and experience a powerful and unexpected source of happiness beyond what we believed possible.

GRATITUDE FOR
THE SEASON

Ah…Christmas! The magic and beauty of it all! Warm jackets, furry gloves, fireplaces, stockings hung for Santa to fill, carols sung and candles lit, decorated trees and presents awaiting beneath to be opened…sometimes even a bit of snow. All these images come to mind as I recall Christmas from my childhood into adulthood. Then came my first Christmas in Florida with my daughter and her family.

As my husband Bob and I arrived at the airport terminal, we were greeted by several people in elf costumes standing by a very tall Christmas tree and handing out candy canes. This was a first for us, as was the message on the monitor nearby that said it was 72 degrees outside. During the following week the temperature went down but not enough to stop us from making Christmas dinner on a grill, wearing shorts and t-shirts, and taking walks after meals without jackets. Not to mention the need for sunglasses everywhere we went, except for one day when the temperature dropped to 58. While Floridians were shivering and looking for sweatshirts and scarves, we were still having ocular challenges from sunlight glinting off the ocean, which we could view from where we were staying.

Though we were having a great time with family, it didn't quite feel like Christmas at first until we went to Celebration City. That's where we saw kids playing in the town square under snowflakes while strolling minstrels sang carols. That seemed more like it should be. Then we learned that what we thought were flakes made from ice were actually made out of soap bubbles. However, everyone, especially the children, was having a glorious time celebrating the holiday in their own way in their own environment and it seemed pointless to let different expectations and remembrances color our experience of this special time with our family. So we joined in whole-heartedly and left our attachment to the past behind. Entering the season with minds open to new ways to celebrate and new eyes to see the joy on the faces of people celebrating with suntanned bodies and sandals, led us to realize that this is truly a season of the heart, and nothing else, which has been the essential message of Christmas since the very beginning.

A SEASON OF THE HEART

Some years ago, quite a few indeed, I clipped the following short list of holiday activities from a magazine. I copied the words into my diary, noting where it came from and the date. It was the time when our children were little, the house was warm and cozy, and we had done quite a bit of decorating, including special lights in the bedroom our two children shared. Jeff was in a crib and Julie was spending her first nights in a small regular kind of bed. I just came across the list again as I was sorting some cards. Not only does it have special meaning to me, it contains the essential message shared during the ministry of a child whose birth has just been celebrated—and it's applicable to everyone, everywhere, all the time.

> This Christmas—or any time
> Seek out a forgotten friend.
> Dismiss suspicion, and replace it with trust.
> Write a love letter. Share some treasure.
> Give a soft answer. Encourage youth.
> Manifest your loyalty in word and deed.
> Keep a promise. Find the time.
> Forgo a grudge. Forgive an enemy.
> Listen. Apologize if you were wrong. Try to
> understand.

Forgo envy. Examine your demands on
others.
Think first of someone else. Be appreciative.
Be kind—be gentle. Laugh a little. Laugh a
little more.
Deserve confidence. Guard against
maliciousness.
Decry complacency. Express your gratitude.
Find your spiritual home. Welcome a
stranger.
Gladden the heart of a child.
Take pleasure in the beauty and wonder of
every day.
Speak your Love. Speak it again. Then
speak it one more time.

No celebration compares with finding the true meaning of
all that is available to use when we extend the best we have
to offer to life itself. The stirring of the heart, followed by
action—then and only then can there be peace in our hearts
and the world. This is the message of the season and the new
year, for those who have the heart and willingness to listen.

God bless us, everyone. You are the expression and the
message and the one giving birth to life's extraordinary
possibilities. It begins with you—and all of us.

THE HAND OF GOD
7/27/20

A woman lies on her stomach in a hospital bed so that her lungs will more easily expel any fluids that gather there. IV's with life-supporting fluids flow into her arms as she attempts to sleep in this unfamiliar and not very comfortable position. Extreme nausea that has plagued her for over a week, begins to ease and breathing doesn't hurt so much anymore. An elevated fever is beginning to work its way down, but indescribable fatigue makes it impossible to turn over in bed without assistance. Staff checks on her every hour, or in between if needed, and through her mind runs the thought that, since she is not yet out of the woods, the uncertainty of where this illness could be heading is very frightening. Having been very healthy up to this point, with enough energy to manage a shoe store, support three at-home teenage children, and take care of necessary business, following all the guidelines to the best of her ability, it's not quite clear how this side-tracking virus made its way into her system, but here it is—confirmed—and with side-effects well in place. Fortunately no need for a respirator at this point, and for that she is very grateful.

On an afternoon when she was more able to do a few things she wrote: "This is a nasty virus. I am VERY fortunate to be heading out of the woods. The fears of and for myself and others are real and complicated. I want to live, as do those I know who had or have cancer, and as do all who have not even faced a life threatening illness, but love their life. We also know of those who have died, from this and many other things. I just keep having to go to God. I may not get what I want, but I will get a measure of peace, clarity and the power to take the next best steps."

On the wall of her private room is a plaque that reads: "You shall serve the Lord your God; He shall bless your bread and water, and I will take sickness from your midst." Exodus 23:25. To which she responded to all the people in our church who have been praying for her recovery:

"Good morning, all! Just when you thought I'm off the prayer list here I am again. As my mom has probably explained, I'm hospitalized with pneumonia as a result of COVID-19. I'm receiving round the clock care from a very nice group of people and am covered in prayer from coast to coast. I am so blessed.

I love the verse from Exodus for its simplicity and because it is from one of my favorite books (I know, I know… that Old Testament…lol!) The cast of characters in Exodus is so varied and complex. There is someone for everyone to relate to in Exodus, in my opinion. God loves and never leaves this crazy bunch and they learn some cool things on an incredible journey, especially the importance of faith and community.

'You at Unity of the Valley are a beautiful faith community that I hold very close in my heart. Keep praying for my lungs so I maybe can sing as good as my mom or any of the fantastic musicians you all have! Blessings—Julie"

This is the Spirit that lives in my daughter, even in the

midst of COVID-19. This is also the Spirit that is assisting her as she returns home today, Sunday, supported with meds, oximeter, new thermometer, breathing exercises, dietary recommendations, a monitor for a quick check in if needed…and the attitude of gratefulness and prayer that never left her, even in her moments of fearfulness. It is also the Spirit that we pay homage to in all we do at Unity of the Valley, and the one that carries us forward into the experience of Wholeness, Faith, Hope, Love and sustainable Joy.

Needless to say it has been quite a week—actually 10 days—for me and my family. We've been all over the map spiritually, emotionally, and as people who are walking in the unknown. Our prayer team, along with the prayer team at Silent Unity, our Elder Council, the church in New Jersey that Laura used to attend, and many congregants here, have been amazingly present. I can't name them all, but I hope you know who you are because it has meant everything to us, and made my days easier. Thank you all from the bottom of my heart. Wow—what a community!!

It will be at least a couple of months before Julie will be able to reach better strength as this virus depletes the body so much and can possibly leave the lungs compromised. However, we know in Truth that all is well, wholeness is possible, and the ever-present Spirit of The One never leaves us.

May you all stay safe, well, and feel the warmth of the Love of the Spirit of Life indwell and infill you.

As Julie signed one of her emails—"That's Love and Lovely".

Sherry

ABOVE THE FLOODPLAIN

I was 9 years old and after a very rainy, indoor kind of morning, I asked my mother if I could walk to my friend's house to spend the afternoon playing paper dolls. (Yes, I was a very girly girl.) It meant walking down a gravel road for about a three block length. What neither my mother nor I knew, was that the small creek that ran beside the road had over flowed and at one point I was facing a very large bit of water that covered the road. I could not ascertain how deep it might be, but even if it had been only 6 inches deep it would have stopped me cold in my tracks, which it did, because I had a real fear of deep water then, and still do now (unless it's in a pool). Yes, I have some overcoming to deal with even at my age.

So I stood there, tears filling my eyes, forgetting that I could just turn back, but also wanting very badly to get to my friend's house. Then I saw my friend's father coming toward me from the other side. He told me to come on because it was not that deep. To me though, it looked deep enough and I did not want to try going through it. Besides, it was visibly flowing from one side of the road to the other and that did not look safe at all. He encouraged me a few more times and then came wading through it to my side.

I thought he was going to carry me, but instead he took my hand and said he would help me. All I could think of was that now my boots would fill with water and my mother would be upset with me. But, because I was embarrassed enough already, I took his hand, closed my eyes and waded across, feeling the water covering at least 2/3 of my dark brown knee high boots.

When we got to my friend's house, he sat me down, helped me off with my boots and shared this wisdom with me. I have never forgotten it. "Your boots were deep enough to keep you safe and dry because someone cared enough to see to it that you had what you needed to go out in the rain. As you get older you will need to be the one to prepare yourself for the deep and scary places of life, by realizing that there is a very big God that is watching over you, loving you, protecting you and sending angels to guide you. Your boots will always be high enough if you take that loving spirit with you everywhere you go, and let go of fear."

Our Unity teachings are so wonderful because they help us realize that a loving Spirit dwells within us and therefore is with us wherever we go, no matter what we face in life. Not only is it within us, we become the outward expression of that Truth when we open our hearts and let the Presence emanate from every cell of our being. In this state of consciousness we rise above the flood plain of life— not matter how shallow or deep—because we have put on the boots of Spirit. Those boots "were made for walkin'" through it all and coming out onto the higher ground prepared for us by a loving creator.

Let's let go of fear, take the hand that is held out to us, and reach out our hand to those around us while sharing Unity's message. Off now to dust my bronzed wading boots.

Love,

Sherry

FROM WHOLE TO HOLE
AND BACK AGAIN

Standing by the mountain stream, I felt such peace and contentment. My husband had just retired and we were celebrating the fact that now we could take those trips, visit those people, do whatever spirit was leading us to do. I remember the words that were pouring into my thoughts "I am whole, I am free and I am unlimited." It was an incredible feeling. And, within a few weeks it all changed.

In the fall, on his birthday in fact, my husband had quadruple by-pass heart surgery. He recovered well and during recovery we altered our travel plans. We would still do some travel, but we would not be as expansive as we had planned on before and as soon as his doctor had given the go ahead words, we would begin. Our first plan was to join our children and their families at our beach place in South Carolina—one family coming down from Virginia and one family coming from Florida. We did that and had a great time. Some other trips, still not expansive, ensued, but we continued to hold out for the Europe one, especially France. We had spent four years in Japan, so we wanted to go in the other direction this time.

It was not to be. When the diagnosis of my husband's Alzheimer's landed in our laps, our plans were organized around what we could do to sustain his health and mind for as long as possible. One airplane trip to see our son was a disaster, so that took care of that and we began focusing on that smaller, but still big, place in our lives. I remember asking, in tears, "Why, God?" and adding "I feel so helpless. What are you doing to us?" Though I had affirmed I had given up defeating and limiting thoughts, many times through the years, they were now staring me in the face again and I felt defeated in so many ways.

Throughout the ensuing years, the narrow focus of being an at-home caregiver, and eventually a daily visitor to his memory care facility, felt like living in a hole. I shared with some friends that the reason they had to repave River Road during that time was because I cried enough tears on the journey back and forth to the facility to wash away even the pavement. And, there were moments of joy, of feeling Spirit's presence, of feeling the energetic bond between my husband and I continuing even when he no longer knew who I was. But it was still a hole, filled with doubt, fear and guilt for not doing and being enough as a person.

His eventual passing was difficult beyond words, of course, but life has opened up again, thanks to some incredible, loving friends who continue to show me what's possible, and I can feel my feet no longer in the muddy hole, but on solid ground. I no longer hold the shovel of disappointment in my hand. In spite of the aging process that presents its challenges, there is an experience of wholeness that has returned. I have a wonderful guide and am being shown the way. I am setting unlimited boundaries and allowing the horizons to continue to broaden.

We all get into holes of disappointment and aborted pleasures, more than once in this lifetime. That can happen at any time and without forewarning, as many of you know. However, when we finally "get it" that we are always connected to the abundant source of goodness, we can begin to see that a hole might have been necessary to slow us down long enough to re-establish the proper connection with that unlimited source.

As I closed the pages on the album of photos of my husband's life, it was with a sigh of relief, knowing that it was as it was. Now it is as it is. My wish for you is that you never get stuck in self-defeating reactions. But knowing you are human, as I am, it is most likely to happen at times. At those times we can stretch out our arms, let the spirit of love embrace us, the Light of The One surround us, and know that the Presence watches over us through our friends, our family and our own intuitive process. Be here now for each other. That makes the biggest difference of all.

THIS IS US

An article in the Oprah magazine about the importance of families caught my eye and heart this week—the week we celebrate the presence of love in our world. The title of the article is "This Is Us" and the descriptive words that followed warmed my mind and body with the realization of their importance. For example:

"If you want to be as happy as the folks on these pages, we'd encourage you to see it [family] for what it can be: a marvelous, occasionally messy collection of partners, parents, exes, siblings, babies and best friends—all bonded by that most power of glue—love."

The reading of this article was preceded by a related experience last Friday evening. I had been invited to share in a meal with a special person, the uncle and friend of a talented young man who was vacationing in his uncle's winter retreat area. The two of them had so much to share, including fond remembrances of their family history, which goes back several generations in their collective memories. What they described directly reflected the "partners, parents, exes, siblings, babies and best friends" expressed in the Oprah article—as do all of our families when we take the time to contemplate our personal histories.

Being present for their discussion—which included so much warmth, humor, acceptance and love—brought home to me once again, this fact: The first place we learn what love is all about is within our families. We learn to receive love and, if conditions exist that nurture that experience, we grow in that love and eventually share it in our own way with those who come into our lives. If love is repressed due to unfortunate incidents or attitudes, it doesn't go away. It hides out in the human heart until something or someone comes along to bring it forth again. I hope and pray that the former happens more often than not and I am sad when it doesn't happen.

I heartily celebrate when we nurture love in our families in such a way that whatever happens within them, we can find solutions that will allow us to put ourselves back together again stronger than before, and continue to hold forth the family constellations, whatever their design may be, as the very ground upon which love is born, shared and allowed to reshape us, our families and our worlds.

Though we may try to define or categorize the supposedly many kinds of love, there is really only one kind of love. That love was put in our hearts by a Divine Source, who knew we would need that compassionate energy to make it through this journey called life. May you, and all of us, remember to keep love alive—in our families, in our friendships, in our partnerships, and in our hearts. There is enough love to go around. What we often do is forget to tell each other of the love we have for them, be they a family member, a sibling, a partner or a good friend. We all need to hear the words "I love you" as often as possible, for whatever reason it is given. I have a friend who likes to capitalize the word Love, even in the middle of sentences, when it is being deeply felt because it shows the feeling was genuine, not lightly tossed about casually. I like that. I've begun to adopt the practice. A well-known song title asks the question: "What Is This Thing Called Love?" I don't have all the answers, but I do know the feeling.

ACROSS THE OCEANS—
CHURCH

"This England" is the name of a magazine I have subscribed to for quite a few years now, ever since my return from a Summer visit to that beautiful, historical and intriguing country. Both the visit and the magazine have sustained my fascination with the English people, their culture, and my family's part in the historical formation of what the magazine refers to as "...our green and pleasant land." I used to dream of going there when a young child and, during WWII, I answered an ad in the newspaper to become a part of the pen pal circle with a child in that country. We have corresponded ever since and that long-term relationship has been a great source of pleasure for both of us.

Janet and I were teenagers together, each in our own cultural way, shared our wedding day experiences, celebrated the birth of our children and comforted each other as our parents left this life. She and her children have been here to visit us in Oregon, and Bob and I have visited them in their small village in England—one of the few villages that still had a Lord of the Manor at that time, who lived in a large manor house that over looked beautiful and ideal fox hunting fields. I felt so at home in that country, but most especially in the town of Canterbury.

However, with all the gorgeous cathedrals of which I never tired visiting, the beautiful Cotswolds we traveled through and the delightful experience of seeing an actual Roman bath with a terrace and enjoying fish and chips wrapped in newspaper lunch afterward—it was the rugged coastlines, the choppy, blue, restless sea that brought my heart up into my throat, filling it with such awe, that made me get down on my knees and thank God for the opportunity to visit this land and experience the beauty of His creation in a place that somehow my soul felt it had lived in before—more than once.

And so, in honor of our Sunday topic for June 5—"Our Connection with Oceans" I am sharing this poem from my favorite magazine with you:

MY CHURCH

I do not see my church in rules and
regulations. I see my church in the glory
of creation.
I see my church in God's devotion, in the
towering mountains and the restless ocean.
Church does not have to be made of stone
and clay.
I see my church in a summer garden on a
beautiful day.
And when I look up to the Milky Way, I
find my church by a quiet stream
In a quiet place where I can rest and dream.
I find my church in the valleys and the
hills and when I see the golden daffodils.

Yes, I find my church in all creation. God's
power beyond imagination

—by Arthur S. Magee

Now, having said all that, there is plenty of time to worship
in that way after services on Sunday and during all the hours
before Sunday morning at 10:30. There is something about
coming together within stone, clay, lumber, windows, lights,
candles, awesome music and incredible spiritual people that
makes it easier to sing a song of joy to all of the outdoor
creations, including the rugged shores of the Oregon coast
and elsewhere. So…see you on Sunday! Right? I will be carrying with me though, a vial of sea water from the English
shores, to remind me of the epiphany and the inspiration
of one special day in "the green and pleasant land" where
God fully declared to me " Wherever thou art, I am."

It is all a reminder that I really need to get to the Oregon
coast and let the healing waves splash on my bare feet. I am
the bubble, make me the sea.

GLIMPSES OF DIVINE BEAUTY SURROUND US

I can see it clearly and it makes me smile. My good friend with mud on her shoes, gloves on her hands and an intent look on her face, as she leans over a shrub on the edge of her large pond, busily trimming and grooming it with love and caring and knowing exactly what to do to make the soon to be flowering shrub raise its short branches as high as it can to the sky, knowing it has a special place in this garden lovers paradise because one of God's gardeners is here. The gardener's heart is full of joy, in spite of the sneeze that follows an airborne burst of pollen. This is her sanctuary and touching the earth is her healing process, her prayer of gratitude for life.

Another vision comes to mind. Another friend with a walking stick in hand, and his wife beside him breathing in deeply, both appreciating the fresh air in a moment of task-free abandonment. Beside them trot their precious dogs, following their "parents" on an afternoon hike. Flooding over all of them, is that feeling of being in the nature that sustains and uplifts body and soul. Perhaps, the thought is there that says "this is what our world is truly all about— being a garden of Eden created just for us." Sharing it together is a gift in itself and they smile at each other.

And then an apple tree comes to mind. An older tree with a place, about four feet off the ground, where its two main branches part, each to do its individual production of delicious fruit. Seated in the crook of that space is a young girl, book in hand, reading on an early summer day. She glances up to see before her where the hill of her family farm dips and curves enough to provide a breath-taking view of the valley floor below. A floor rich with freshly plowed farm land and distant homes of family friends. The sky is an incredible blue. No clouds at all except for one small puff floating alone over the distant fir trees.

The girl may be young, but somehow, even in her advanced age of the present moment, that scene has never left her mind, nor the feeling that swept over her when she realized she was a part of it all and so blessed by the gift of its beauty, and permanence, and peace because yes, there is a loving, understanding creator who provides beauty beyond comprehension. When her mother calls out the kitchen window to let her know that lunch is ready, she reluctantly hops down out of the tree, closes her book and decides to tell her mother about it all. But over the bowl of homemade noodle soup, there are no words and so she keeps the thoughts to herself. A treasure laid up in the kingdom of her heart to sustain her when walking through the rough places in life.

"The Awe Inspiring Beauty of Life" is our theme for this coming Sunday, and what better way to receive that inspiration than to share in it with friends. And what better way to experience the truth of the topic than to breathe the air, smell the flowers, sit in the shade of trees, fish in the streams, or hike the mountain trails and feel the joy and freedom of our beautiful planet. Then, on days when snow falls or rain pounds the roof, to sit and view from the window in the warmth of our homes, the continuing unfoldment of the beauty we behold. As we take it in, we can feel the blood pulsing in our veins, and the warmth of our breath and know we are a part of it all and that is just plain incredibly amazing. Thank you, God. We are humbled.

A PRAYER FOR
FATHER'S DAY

Our Father who art in the kitchen, on the playground, in the nursery, on the job.

Hallowed be thy name. Be it Bill, John, David or Ibrahim, Pierre, Vladimir, Toshi, Hans or Alani –or any other name heard round the globe.

Thy Kingdom is come, thy will is being done -

Through the standing tall, and stooping low to tie a shoelace, through the extended hand, smiling eyes, and shoulder to cry on.

Through income earned, and grass well mowed—and hammer and nail, and stitches sewed with unsteady hand on the ear torn off on a teddy bear's head.

Through the gentle carrying to bed a sleeping child who's pillow waits his/her head, through time spent listening as the beloved teen unleashes, in fear and frustration, how the world and life, in general, is too much to bear.

Thy will is done. On earth as decreed in heaven—through the father who raises his children while all the angels sing the praise of one so brave as to take it on in one very short time span of life. One who partners with a mother in the doing, or does it alone.

Father, you *give us each our daily bread*—the bread of

your love, your caring, your strength, your nurturing; even when we see confusion or uncertainty on your face, we know it is because you are figuring out how to make the loaf of your willingness sustain us when we need the nourishment of your wisdom so we may grow into the person you would have us be.

Father, forgive us when we become demanding and rebel at the need to be contained and turned in our thinking to right purpose. Through you we learn how to *forgive others* by the example of your forgiving heart, the drying of our tears, and the turning of spilled milk into laughter while sharing in the clean-up.

We walk *daily in temptation* as we assert our independence. You show us how to not stay there, but instead teach us to move on. By your example we turn the rough and tough challenging times into *you deliver us from our humiliation* and teach us to believe in ourselves.

Yours is the kingdom but you let it be ours as well. You have the power, but you infuse it in us and with your strength set our foot along life's path so we may see the glory and beauty of the life before us.

Forever and ever, we are in your debt, though you will not take anything in return. For this we honor you, *we give you the glory* and prepare to care for you when the time comes that we can be by your side walking with you in the late years of our incredible life.

Our father, thou are the art of heaven No matter who you are, no matter what you have done or left undone, no matter how long you are with us—or not with us. It is you who, with our mother, brought us into this world and gave us life so that we may have it eternally ongoing when we continue our unfoldment as spiritual beings.

Our father—who art in each room of the house of our growing up and at each corner of the twists and turns that come on our life path, we *feel the sacredness of your connection with us.* Even if we never saw your face, or watched it disappear from our view and never understood why—whoever you are, you are our father. In reverence we speak your name.

WALKING ON WATER

I lay very still in the hospital bed waiting for my mind to focus and my mouth to stop saying silly things to the doctor who was checking in on me. "The meds will wear off soon. We needed to give you a little booster shot to get you ready for this." With that he gestured toward the door through which the nurse came carrying a little bundle wrapped in a pink blanket. "Here's your little daughter. Congratulations!" she said with a smile as I reached up to receive the new life I had delivered into the world just a few short minutes ago.

As my daughter was placed into my arms I asked, "Has her father seen her yet?" This was in the 1960's and things were done differently back then. "No," said the doctor "but I am going to go get him right now. He knows she is here, though and is he ever excited." As he exited, I noticed the fatigue on his face. The nurse told me he had delivered 7 babies so far and the day was not over yet. "Your little girl was number 1000 in his career so far. "Wow, really?," I commented. "Yes, and we all think he can walk on water because he loves every one of them and tells them they are welcome to this world."

Walk on water. At that time I was deep into my Lutheran phase (I've had several phases before Unity) and so I naturally thought of the story of Jesus walking on the water when he went to join his disciples in the boat. I looked down at Miss Julie Angela, and said "Hi there. I think that if it is needed, you will have no trouble with doing that. Just look at you." She was staring at me very intently with her big brown eyes, and her full head of dark hair all slicked back with a soft curl at the sides, she looked adorable. Little did I know at that time, that the day would come when she would indeed need to reach out to save a "sinking ship" and as a result, learn how to walk on water and be successful in the rescue.

That little girl is now in her 50's and after a tragic series of events, and without me being present except by phone and some visits, has had to turn everything she has, is and hoped to be, over to a power greater than herself so that she could survive the turmoil and chaos, the disappointment and heartbreak, and the unknown future resulting from two completely unexpected events in her life.

One was the abandonment of six adopted biracial children by a father who could not understand his role in helping to raise the children he agreed to help walk through this world and therefore gradually faded from view. Second was the incarceration of one of her children after an unfortunate event that followed a teenage confrontation in which he was trying to protect his friends. This last week, in spite of the best of lawyers, the jury declared him guilty of something he did not do, though he was on the scene. My daughter will now continue to be faced with jail visits and encouraging her 16 year old son to keep the faith. After a year and a half of having all freedoms taken away while waiting to be tried, the young man will continue to reach out his hands to the mother as she does her best to calm the storm.

Through all of this, the once little girl has had to be provider of necessities, counselor, daytime elementary teacher, classroom assistant for special needs children, homework drill sergeant, taxi driver, neighbor, babysitter, errand runner, cook, laundress, tutor, window washer, clothes mender, floor scrubber, support for her mother who was caring for her father who had Alzheimer's—and everything else required of her—and now adding jail visits to her agenda. This has necessitated the putting aside of her writing, of which she is very talented, an incredible photographer, and time for the establishing of a potential relationship. Through it all she has never relented on her faith in a Divine Spirit and has grown to be a true woman of substance.

And so, Mother's Day is almost here and her journey continues. I have saved every letter and card she has written and every email, because this is a life story, already, of someone of whom so much has been asked. When Spirit inquired "Who shall we send to do the work?" she could have turned away, but instead she took a deep breath, cried many tears, asked for relief, yet still answered, "Here I am. I will do it, because I love my children."

This, in my opinion, is what walking on water in human form can look like sometimes. Instead of running away, giving up, or collapsing under the pressure of the demand put on us we somehow find the strength to "carry on." I have had the privilege of talking with so many right here in this congregation who are already taking the walk. To whom much is given, much is expected.

When Jesus was walking on water he was going out to be of help. His power came from a deep source and was part of the fulfillment of his purpose in his brief lifetime. Sometimes we are called on to rise up to that spiritual place where, while never easy, we can meet the demands placed upon us. I so wish that wasn't so for my daughter. It weighs on my heart often. Yet watching her rise to the occasion(s), always walking in faith while "hanging in there" and through it all teaching me so much about faith, strength, beauty, and unconditional love. She is stretching me in every way, calling me up higher and higher. Is she perfect? Of course not. None of us are on all levels, but she is getting darn close. No doubt many of you feel the same way about some of the women in your lives.

AN UNUSUAL
LOVE STORY

My new found friend Jimmy was with me for almost
a week. He was such a good listener, and disturbed
very little within the house, or within my life. He was just
there, sitting with me on various occasions and, in his quiet
way, I could feel his presence even when he was in some
other room of the house, though I could not always tell
which room it was because of his quiet demeanor. He did
not need to wear a mask, which is a good thing because
I didn't have one small enough to fit him. I did not need
to wear a mask because I did not feel his breath, if he
breathed at all, would have much impact on the quality of
the air within my house. And so, we were content to share
space without concern and do our own thing, in our own
individual way.

I met Jimmy on a sunny afternoon when I had my
deck-side door open. He didn't knock. He just very quietly
entered and took his place beside the screen door and then,
without demands of any kind, took residence in my living
room, on the piano bench. I was puzzled about his presence,
but quite flattered when I moved to where he was and he
didn't move. He just allowed me to be there. His face was
not one on which a person could detect a smile, if indeed

there was one, but I had a smile on mine when I held out my hand he allowed the gesture. He didn't move when I then gently placed a finger beside his small body, in a gesture of friendship.

I told him it was fine with me if he stayed around for a while, which he did for almost a week, as I mentioned. While here he followed me almost everywhere I went and always sat close to me when I would allow him, which I learned to do without any concern at all. He was surprisingly calm and enjoyable, peaceful and quiet.

He left just as quiet as he came. I did not know of his leaving, not hear any sounds of departure. When I told a good friend of mine about Jimmy, my friend shared with me that most likely Jimmy was just as curious about me as I was about him, wanted to get to know me and be my friend… and maybe, in his own unusually quiet way, wanted to have a good life just like me. I like that thought and have carried those words with me when I have the opportunity to interact, observe, or take photos of some of the varied and wonderful species that abound in the world around us. I have also, since Jimmy's days of companionship, retired the swatter that hung by the side of my stove in the kitchen. Amazing what the slowdown of a virus related, isolated life can do to one's perspective and vision. In my cabin-feverish mind, I was actually able to tell Jimmy how he had taught me about Love in a new and different way.

The thoughts shared with me by my friend, the practice of unconditional acceptance of all forms of life, of which I am a part in my own unique way—as are you—has intensified the feelings of deep Appreciation and Love for this life I/we have been given the opportunity to experience. I remember a Buddhist teacher I sat with during my ministerial school days who smiled at my impatience with a group of mosquitos that were buzzing around my arm. I have attracted mosquitos all of my life and been treated for infections from their bites more than once. The teacher shared with me how to do a brief meditation to keep them from bothering me. I was amazed at how it worked and have used it successfully several times since then. Maybe you already know about it. Like the species Jimmy represented, the silly little mosquitos are something we have to put up with, so why not learn what we can from them. I know, that sounds a bit strange. (Consider the source. Ha ha) Also consider using my friend's wise words whenever you/we can as a good exercise in how changing one's perspective can change any experience we may have. I need this lesson more and more these days and I believe the whole world does, too.

On Sunday we will celebrate the day of Love-ing that appears on our calendar every year. It's a wonderful day to enjoy all the things it has to offer by way of celebration. I sometimes wonder what Jesus and other great teachers would have to say about roses, cards and chocolates, etc., etc. if they were here for this upcoming day. Perhaps they would approve since the more we focus on love, in all its forms, the more positive energy we share with the world. Love is our nature. Love is real. Love is healing. Love is Joy. God is Love. We can Love even while apart, for Love knows no distance—it dwells in the heart.

Celebrating

———∞∞∞———

"When you arise in the morning, think of what a precious privilege it is to be alive, to breathe, to think, to enjoy, to love."

—Marcus Aurelius

ANYWHERE ALONG
THE WAY

Several times this week, the following short story has come my way. I don't know its origin, but it caught my attention and perhaps you have read it, too. I would like to share once again however, because of the beauty of its message. It goes like this:

> A professor gave a balloon to every student, asked them to inflate it, write their name on it and throw it into the hallway. Then the professor mixed up all the balloons and the students were given five minutes to find their own balloon. Despite a hectic search, no one found their own balloon. At that point the professor told the students to take the first balloon they found and hand it to the person whose name was written on it. Within 5 minutes everyone had their own balloon. The professor then said to them, "These balloons are like happiness. We will never find it if everyone is looking for their own. But, if we care about other people's happiness... we will find ours, too.

During these times of uncertainty, there may come that moment when the feeling of happiness is elusive. We might even begin to loose trust in an all providing Divine Spirit of harmony and well-being because that voice feels silenced within us.—Maybe not silenced entirely, depending on the challenges we face, but even if momentarily, we begin to wonder how do we return to the place of peace and joy as quickly as possible?

Just the other day I was walking in my favorite park, feeling a little less than happy because my family members are all so far away and, for various reasons we are all aware of, we will not be gathering together to celebrate the holidays this year. It would be nice to be a migrating goose who can fly above all this that is going on and I shared this with my duck friends in the park, some of whom I have now named, and they seemed to understand. I am so blessed by them.

While I took a break from my walk and sat for a moment, a family with two children walking by stopped to chat for a minute. One of the children, perhaps noticing my white hair, asked, "Are you a Grandma or a Great Grandma?" "I am both," I responded. "What is your name,?" I was asked. I replied, "Sherry". The parents then asked me a few questions about my family, thought it was "cool" to see me out enjoying the park. They asked about my family and the holidays. When I shared circumstances, one of the children reached into their pocket and then handed me a Hershey's foil wrapped chocolate kiss. I accepted and we all laughed together. They did not conclude with the usual "Good to see you," but with an amazing "Hoping you will be happy in spite of everything. Continue to take good care of yourself. Happy holidays." Then one of the kids said, "Bye, Grandma Sherry." Someone cared about my happiness. What a gift! What a difference in my day!

In the first Christmas card I received this year there was this New Year's inclusion statement: " It is important to remember that the beginning can be anywhere along the way. " The beginning can be found even on a walkway in a park...the beginning of renewed, remembered and re-experienced happiness. And the commitment to, once again, pass happiness along to others as often as possible.

I may not have family close by right now, and special friends are missing from sight, but it has been well said that where there is love, there is no distance. Also—True friends are never apart. Only in distance, but not in the heart. It is with joy and gratitude in my heart that I pass this special greeting from Christmas card number two—may this knowing bring you some happiness:

"If not for you, someone who needed love would have gone without it.

There would have been one less smile, one less laugh, one less hug

And the song of life might have skipped a beat.

If not for you, something special would be missing.

The sun is out as I finish this. It is now a whole 53 degrees outside. Time to head for the park again. I need to check in with some ducks that live there, and maybe there will be someone to share a greeting with, too.

Let the warmth of life wash over you.

Sherry

A BED BY THE WINDOW

———≈———

Starting off with a bit of humor because it is such a good metaphor for life right now:

"During a visit to my doctor, I asked him, 'How do you determine whether or not an older person should be put in an old age home?'

He replied, 'We fill up a bathtub, then we offer a teaspoon, a teacup and a bucket to the person and ask them to empty the bathtub.'

'Oh, I understand.' I said. 'A normal person would use the bucket because it is bigger than the spoon or teacup.'

'No,' he said. 'A normal person would pull the plug. Do you want a bed near the window?"

We seem to be at a place right now, where we cannot seem to find the bigger, more creative, and often obvious answers to some things. Or even know where to look for them because "normal" isn't normal anymore. Maybe it never was, but it sure felt that way. I know I long for something I can't even describe and I want to return to that "normal" as soon as possible to see if it was lost there somehow. But, let's face it, we never will. No matter what world, country, or personal events have happened in our lives, the outcome of any return to normalcy has always looked different, due mainly to the fact that in the process, we ourselves had changed as well. For me, the change that has happened has caused me to be less like my true self than at any other time in my life. I'm comfortable sharing that because so many others have shared that it is happening with them, too. I don't always feel "normal" and I certainly don't always respond that way sometimes.

It has been suggested that we have become polarized within ourselves, within our country and within the world as a whole. An atheist friend of mine admitted that we "could sure use that anticipated Christian Second-coming to happen now. Rome isn't burning—yet," he said – " but if there is a second-coming that will rescue us from any conflagration it needs to be now." If not, he mentioned the potential that we would either explode or end up on a bed staring out the window while trying to figure it out. A little dire, I admit, but laying in bed longer in the mornings sometimes, while pondering what the day could look like, feels a bit like that. He, and I are ready for something better. Maybe not all of you, but I'll bet some of you are

How do we start this return—both on a larger scale and then in our own personal lives? Thich Nhat Hanh suggests this rather radical approach for the larger scale of the world:

"The situation of the world is like this. People completely identify with one side, one ideology. To understand the suffering and the fear of a human being who thinks different, we have to become one with him or her. To do so is dangerous-we will be suspected by both sides. But if we don't do it, if we align ourselves with one side or the other, we will lose our chance to work for peace. Reconciliation is to understand both sides. From this we can find the common ground, which has begun to be talked about recently in articles, media and other places. This means pulling the plus, as mentioned in the beginning humor piece, pulling the plug on many places where we are stuck and beginning again.

On the smaller scale of our personal lives, these are steps from an article titled "*How To stay Young.*" (unknown)

- Throw out nonessential numbers. These include age, weight and height. Let the doctors worry about them. That is why you pay them.

- Keep cheerful friends. The grouches will pull you down.

- Keep learning. Never let the brain idle. Do whatever to keep it active. And idle mind will atrophy.

- Freedom unused will also atrophy so allow freedom to flourish everywhere.

- Enjoy the simple things. Laugh often, long and loud until you gasp for breath.

- Let the tears happen. Grieve and then move on. The only person who is with us our entire lives is us. Be ALIVE while you are alive.

- Surround yourself with what you love. Your home is your refuge.

- Cherish your health. If it is good, preserve it. If it is unstable, improve it. If it is beyond what you can improve, get help.

- Don't take guilt trips. Take a trip to the mall, to the next county, to a foreign country—but, not to where guilt is.

- Tell the people you love, that you love them at every opportunity you have.

On the days when none of this works, then go ahead, take that bed by the window, (be sure there is a window to look out of), pull the plug on all that stuff inside and let it drain out quickly until all is clear. No need to hang on to anything. Then let yourself be filled with Spirit's Love. When full, call up someone, or tell someone in person that they are loved. Bet you will hear the same back from them. People need to hear it.

My bed is by a window and tonight, weather permitting, I will be able to see the full moon. So reassuring in its constant cycling. I may go outside and let it shine down on me as I have a treasure in my heart that needs a blessing of reassurance.

From the window of Life.

Sherry

AT ONE WITH THE RIVER

When I was in ministerial school, one of the ministers from the church I attended on Sundays told the following story. It's about both affirming what you want or know to be true, and being careful what you ask for. It is also about learning to live in the moment.

As the small group left the church to go to a nearby river to enjoy an afternoon of rafting and kayaking, the minister had some apprehensions about the actual experience of being in the water as she was not always comfortable with a moving stream. But since she had been invited, enjoyed the people's company, and liked the idea of a group from church getting together, it seemed like the right thing to do. To facilitate her blending with the group in a positive way she prayed the following prayer: "Lord, make me one with the river, so that I can feel its gift." She affirmed it many times, including when the leader of the group was helping her put on her life-jacket and when she was getting into the small four passenger boat.

Clutching the sides of the boat until she felt comfortable with the flow of the river, her hands began to get very tired from the grip and she put them on her knees. At that moment the boat hit a rough spot in the water, turned around, got caught up in a swirling eddy and then began to spin again. Without any advance notice she and one of the other passengers were tossed out of the boat and were drawn fairly quickly down the river. Just as fear began a very tight grip on her whole being, a branch from the banks along the side appeared reaching out over the water. She clung to it until she was rescued by the second boat that was following them. As she slid into the boat, dripping wet and shaking, it came to her that what she should have requested in her prayer was, "Lord, make me one with the boat."

She shared with us that, in preparation for the trip, and the brave attempt to step out of her comfort zone, it would have been helpful to also pray for a release of fear so that when she got to the river, her restless, anxious mind, would be calm enough to fully relax into the experience. She had not done that, but instead, had been concerned about how she would be observed by the congregants who invited her, how she would manage getting into the boat looking like she knew what she was doing, and several other things that kept her from being able to release tension that could not allow full enjoyment of the experience.

I experience a restless mind more often than I would like to admit. After thirty years as a classroom teacher and twenty-two years as a minister, plus eight years of caregiving for my husband who had Alzheimer's, my restless mind has a hard time letting go of the need to control things so that they come out perfectly for everyone. It has often kept me from fully experiencing and appreciating where I am or what I am doing. Fortunately, over the past year, I have had a wonderful teacher who has shown me another way of experiencing each moment of each day, and I'm learning to trust and allow the days to unfold in a more natural way, sometimes hour by hour. My gratitude for these lessons, and the very patient teacher (who shall remain nameless) is eternal. I have not been an easy student to work with by any means.

So, my desire for YOU, is to allow yourself to stand on the bank of the river, be it a river of flowing water, or the river of life itself, and observe its flow. Let it teach you, through the Spirit of life itself embedded within the expression of YOU, how to fully experience and appreciate what is being shared with you, told to you, expressed to you, in all the myriad forms that are provided as channels to reach our hearts, souls and minds. All are offered as a blessing for us. The universe is on our side and waiting for us to slow down long enough to breathe in its wonders. All blessings are full of love and grace and are meant to honor our very existence, our being-ness, our human-ness and our divinity. What an amazing gift!

THE UNFORGETTABLE
NOW MOMENT

The sun has set over the cottage, but the flow of the still-lighted horizon casts an aura of peaceful warmth inviting walkers to step onto the garden path and stroll slowly so as to savor the beauty of the evening. Autumn leaves float soundlessly onto the shadows cast by small birch trees, and plants are still full of blooms as if it were July instead of October. A gong sounds in the east end of the garden, followed by wind chimes and the sound of a waterfall—an opportunity to put aside cares of the day and step into the now moment.

Stepping into the now moment may be a bit of a stretch for some of the strolling guests, but not for the family members whose hands they hold or whose wheelchairs they push. Silent in the wonder of it all, those being walked and wheeled, have eyes opened wide, as if seeing each beautiful images for the first time, and one is heard to say, "Oh so beautiful." Another said, "He likes being outside." "He" is the pronoun used to refer to himself. It takes place of "I," because "I" has no meaning anymore as the sense of the egoic has begun to fade into obscurity—not into memory, because memory is not available anymore. One is fully in the present teaching the "pushers" and the "hand holders" what it means to be only there.

Such is the way it was, recently, on a beautiful evening in a gorgeous garden at a place where those with fading memories live and are cared for and where family members gather to adjust to a new way of living in the now moment, a place where silence is spoken more often than a plethora of words. A place where, beyond belief, one can, in the midst of personal sadness, experience a deeply gratifying walk if one is willing to let go and become one with the experience. There is no deeper place of Now than here where there is no time. There is only God.

Eckhart Tolle, in his book *The Power of Now* said it well: *How to stop creating time? Realize deeply that the present moment is all you ever have. Make the Now the primary focus of your life.* And he also wrote *Silence is a potent carrier of Presence. To listen to the silence, wherever you are, is an easy and direct way of becoming present*

A SUNSET TO
CELEBRATE

Three common sayings about growing older:

1. You're only as old as you feel.

2. Growing old is for sissies.

3. I don't know what to say. I've never been this old before.

And then, from a gentleman sitting on the side of a brick planter at 5th Street Market: *"The Golden Years" lured a lot of us into thinking there was truth in that statement so we fell for it. I've got gold in my teeth, none in my pocket. But in my head, where I live a lot now, there is so much that blesses me.*

For many of us, the realization that we are now "older" has brought with it the big question, "When did this happen? It sure snuck up on me." And, from the musical *Fiddler on the Roof*—"Sunrise, sunset, swiftly flow the years. I don't remember growing older. When did she (they)?"

Yet, there is so much beauty in the later years of life. Releasing of the "doing" and easing into the "beingness" of life. Renewal of old friendships, watching grandchildren grow, laughing at the adventures of younger years and all the foibles and craziness, and the silliness of all we thought was the real stuff of life. "Do you remember when…?" Followed by hours of laughter at ourselves. Photo albums, love, births, travels—and then the quiet reconnections to the Spirit of the Holy that has been part of our experience and is now intensifying in its all-embracing presence.

NEW

This morning is so full: new fence being erected in spite of a rain shower or two, awning company here to give a bid, X-rays being scheduled, friend bringing by grocery items, yard care people, and a clogged bathtub drain…and it's 11 a.m. Just took a look in the mirror and realized I am still in the muumuu that covers my jammies, which I had to put on very quickly because the fence guys were here at 8 a.m. sharp. I had not known which day they were coming for sure and I needed to speak with them through my glassed-in screen door. Communications are being done by text as well since we can't meet outside face-to-face.

With eyes a little glazed over, I plopped onto a chair planning to take some calm-down moments, but as I did the phone rang. Oh no, I thought…how can this be? And, as Divinity has a way of responding, it turned out to be a call from a Unity of the Valley angel who wanted to know how I was doing and to let me know I was being thought about. We talked for about 20 minutes and it was such a blessing that I came away refreshed and with a grateful heart. It brought to mind a quote from a special friend of mine that came at the end of an email: "There is always room to feel some Happy." Words of importance from this friend are always capitalized. I enjoy that.

All of this made me realize that though there is a huge difference between choosing to be alone or with yourself, compared to being forced to be alone without much choice. That, I feel, is at the center of what many of us are going through these days. We like to have choices and yet, for a bit of time, we are asked to put those aside in the best interest of the collective whole. That's what it means when we say, "We are all in this together." Of course, as we are learning, there are many ways to be "together." I still prefer a balance between physically together and individually alone. Many of you have other people in your house to interact with. I hope you realize what a blessing that is—I'm sure you do.

During the past six weeks I have felt the disappointment and angst of being forced to be alone more often than is comfortable for me. This includes driving my car. I like driving to do errands, but when it is social time, I like being in the car with someone else. I treasure those times so much. Bottom line, I can be alone for fairly long periods as long as I can also get out and socialize frequently enough to make being alone for a while feel good.

"Happiness is a state of being we can access regardless of who we are with or not with, as long as we are truly with ourselves." -Tanya Davis. I've been with myself for quite a number of years now and while I like myself and enjoy conversations with myself, for me there is nothing like sitting outside a restaurant and sharing a meal with someone, or visiting in a park, or taking a walk together and just exchanging energy and ideas. I wonder how many of you feel the same way? I have a friend who says that being alone is her preferred way of being, plus that means she doesn't have to get dressed and go somewhere. I could take a lesson from her—maybe—but it's just not who I am, so I have to live with it.

All I really want to say this week is that whatever is going on for each of us does not go unnoticed by Spirit, is supported by the love of that Spirit, and that Spirit (call it God or whatever you will), had a reason for making more than one of us. And, since that is true, then in all our individuality we become a collective whole—a group of people called to support each other in our own way. This seems especially true now as our well-populated earth globe upon which we live and from which we draw our substance and sustenance, journeys through a difficult stretch. I'm trying my best, as I know you are.

Would that it could be different, and in time it will. Yet when this major challenge is over, the world will not be what we remember it to be, no matter what. We need to be aware of that, ready for what that means, and give it all over to Spirit. As we do this, may we remember to love without condition and beyond expectation, while we open ourselves to being there for each other, not only through this time now, but in the days ahead.

Remember, too: "There is always room to feel some Happy."

THE SPACES BETWEEN

When my family and I were living in Japan and my husband and I were teaching at the American School just outside of Tokyo, we traveled back and forth together as a family between our small apartment and the school. It was not unusual to see on one part or the other of those trips, a line of kindergarten students, in their regulated blue uniforms and yellow hats, traveling either to or from their school. They always walked in line behind their teacher and we were always amazed at how they never veered from that formation and kept a seemingly expected space between each other. When crossing streets they kept that line and rarely did we see the teacher having to turn around to check on their little ones. We often commented about how disciplined those little ones were at such an early age.

One of the first things we saw upon our return to the states, in a similar scenario, was a line of young ones following their teacher, with a helper walking along beside them and each child hanging onto a rope of some kind, held by the teacher. We didn't know if that rope was for safety or as a visible and tactful sign of the need for directions to be followed. What we did notice is that upon viewing lines of students at other times, keeping little ones together presented a kind of challenge that often required two or three people managing the line of adorable little ones.

Different cultures, different lifestyles, different ways of managing kid traffic in the concern for safety. In one culture kids learning very early how to conform and even keep appropriate distance between themselves and others without having to be reminded. In the other culture, freer spirits knowing where they were heading, but independently attempting to get there in their own personal fashion and style and needing a bit more guidance to stay well protected. Both styles appropriate for their culture. All of them in both groups loved and treasured by the adults who cared for them

So, here we are today, in the midst of a "crisis" and as adults we are having to "line-up" in ways we have never had to before. Some of us following the rules that are handed down to the maximum—others doing the best they can while continuing to claim the freedom to do it their way. Yet, we are being called upon to meet the crisis in a particular way so as to curb the spread of a potential long-lived and dangerous virus. How we line up, how we face this, how we respond, both physically, mentally and emotionally is not only extremely important, but also urgent. The big question is, not how long will this last (though that question is ever present in my mind) but the bigger question is can we do what we are asked to do to shorten the distance between confinement and the freedom to go back to leading our lives in the way we all prefer and treasure?

My hope is that we can all, for this crucial time, do what we have to do with the willingness to walk without having to be dragged along, and to do it side by side—one heart, one mind, one desire, one hope. No, I don't agree with all of the requirements as I do have the maturity and intelligence to be wise on my own. But here we are... We have people who are leading and guiding that have more knowledge that I do, (I know—maybe not all) but we can overcome the negativity, the doubts and fears, the need to panic, and together step into the caring and sharing in so many creative ways that reach across lines and boundaries and cultures that is possible now and move into an incredible global spirit of oneness. It could completely change how we do business, show up, and create the world that will follow.

One of my favorite sayings is: No need to fear the future because God is already there. At this moment it is already tomorrow in other parts of the world and I believe that Spirit is already there, guiding and leading through it all. No, I don't know why viruses are allowed to develop and flourish. I just know that I need you and want you walking with me through this unknown territory. I can't and don't want to do it alone.

CULTURAL
DIFFERENCES

A good friend and I, engaged in a conversation over the phone, were sharing our remembrances of years of teaching together and pondering whether or not, now that we were retired, if we had yet found the true meaning of life. Surely in these supposedly "golden years" it should have become clear. As I shared some thoughts, my friend shared how, in his culture, which is somewhat different than mine, there is one bit of philosophy and teaching that helps to answer that question.

"In your culture," he said, "as you mature you have focused on what life means in general along with what it means to you. In our culture we ask, and we teach our children to ask, What does life, and our life mean in relation to the whole of existence, including the earth, the stars, the seasons, the universe, etc.? We train them to savor the very blood that flows through their veins and then understand it's vital role in everything from caring for the very seeds in the ground to the honoring of the heavens. When one understands that they are part of the whole, it is easier to find and understand one's place in it. This is beyond the limited thinking of "what is the meaning of life" which is often limited to the answer of "I don't know." We teach our children to know from the perspective of their role in the whole, not just themselves."

This reminded me of the time in my kindergarten class when, as was my yearly practice, we were putting on a musical play for the parents. The theme was the sea and I let the children choose what they wanted to be. They chose the usual—fish, turtles, starfish, and two wanted to be seaweed because they liked "slimy, icky things". I had them stand by groups—fish over here, turtles over there, starfish there, and seaweed over there. Two little girls, twin sisters, did not move. I questioned them and their reply was a complete, and unforgettable realization: "We want to be bubbles." When I asked why, they said, "because bubbles help all the animals breathe." Two little, adorable young girls who already understood how to make connections beyond the literal, visible vision we are often limited to, and become part of the greater whole. The sea is not just water and animals. Life is not just you and me. The sea contains part of the rest of the universe. The life we live is like that—part of the whole cosmos and if we, in our daily lives are needed to be, metaphorically, bubbles, or breezes, or infinitesimal things so as to bring ourselves into living in relation to the whole life, then what a privilege to be part of the connection to all things in that way.

When we understand that our roots are not just where we plant our feet, but extend far into the universe and it's galaxies, then life becomes even more precious and we fly on the wings of Spirit to take our place in it. Everything we do and are affects the whole. It's like that scientific understanding that when a butterfly flaps its wings in California it affects the weather in New York. The meaning of our lives is not just about us, but how we are connected to the whole of life everywhere and our place in that wholeness. When we understand this, then we can fly like the eagle and view the whole of all we are connected to and life's meaning is no longer in question.

THE RIGHT
DESTINATION

"Life is often lived as if we are on a train, focused mostly on getting to the 'right' destination. How different could this be if we treated it more like a sailboat ride, checking the winds each day and learning to go with the flow?" (Lorena Smith)

I had to smile at this analogy. Mainly because I love trains and am very uncomfortable in the water and on the water, even in large cruise lines. I like my feet on solid ground at a manageable height because I suffer from altitude sickness at anything over 4500 feet. As you can guess, I'm not much fun to travel with if you are an adventurous, mountain climbing person, and would be a disastrous companion on an around the world cruise.

Yet, I have managed to live with myself in spite of these quirks and one of my favorite objects is a model of a three masted schooner that sits on my desk. It gives me a sense of freedom every time I gaze at it, and the vastness of uncharted seas with nothing to box one in is soothing...like being at the ocean, meditating while seated on the sand. I guess I am an enigma. But, I think we all are. And that's ok.

The wonderfully freeing question, suggested by our guest speaker this coming Sunday (Lorena Smith) is this:

"Remember to ask yourself this question each morning: What do I want to experience today?" (Thank you, Lorena, I love that question) With that as food for our thoughts in the morning, it won't really matter which vessel we choose to convey us through life, or on that day, especially since we will need more than one conveyance at various times throughout the course of our days, depending on what we want to accomplish.

What matters is that we are free to choose, to stop judgment of right and wrong for ourselves and others. Free to move into the most beautiful, pure experience of being fully present to life, knowing there is a higher power that guides our journey. That power is within us, placed there by a creator who gave us the compass of safety in all directions when we allow it to assist us in aligning ourselves with the flow of our innate wisdom, do our best to make wise choices along the way, and let love be the heavenly star that we follow to our destination, whatever it is to be for us.

Today I rode the train, as my destination was to get certain things accomplished. Tomorrow I will sit back in my boat (while it rests on the sand ☺), stare out at the vastness of the sea and let all be in the flow, which I can feel in my heart. Next week? Don't know yet. Spirit has something fun planned, I'm sure. But I will consciously ask "What do I want to experience today?" and then let Spirit go to work.

RETURNING HOME

Nelson Mandela wrote: "There is nothing like returning to a place that remains unchanged to find the ways in which you have altered."

This rang true for me last summer when I went to the rural area where I grew up, drove up the hill I used to climb after getting off the school bus, to trudge home, rain or shine, to our house on the top of the hill. I turned right and noticed that the very short gravel road now had a name, as posted on a new pole by the county. It said "Ripplewood Drive.". Ripple was my maiden name and Wood was our neighbors last name. I had to smile a bit because to call the road by the more elite sounding name that ended with the word "Drive" did not in any way indicate the bumps, the rocks and the dust that I remember blowing across it, not to mention the dry weed on the roadside. But, the house was still there. The one my father built from the ground up way back in the late 40's when we left Portland to become farmers. The house had hardly changed at all. Only the poplar trees had gotten huge and someone had built a horse barn where our garden used to be. And someone else's name was on the mailbox.

I felt myself tearing up a bit, because I knew that though I was part of the "founding family" of this farm and house, I could not go back again. I wanted to tear open the locked gate, march right up to the house and tell who ever was there to get out—this is my home, my place, my farm, I needed to be there again. But there was no one home at that time—and that was a good thing, because I was then able to return to a more rational state and realize, no—this is not mine anymore and even if I were to come back, I am not the same person. Truly, I could not do this again—and I don't really want to. Some of me is still there. My foot prints in the soil somewhere. The young person with dreams, some of which still lie in my heart. But that is not a bad thing because we just can't do everything we want to do in one lifetime—or so I am discovering. But, what has unfolded throughout my life has taken me way beyond what I could have ever imagined in my limited view way back then. And I am very grateful.

Marianne Williamson shared: "It takes courage to endure the sharp pains of self-discovery, rather than choose to take the dull pain of unconsciousness that would then last the rest of our lives". I had to leave the farm. I had to find what else was there for me, just like most of you have had to do; to venture out so as to discover that there is so much more to us that we ever imagined. We can't do this by standing still in one place. "You will never be able to find yourself if you're lost in your old self or in someone else's version of you." (unknown)

I carry in my billfold a saying from Lao Tzu that reads: "At the center of your being you have the answer. You know who you are and you know what you want." One of my high school teachers gave this to me, and it showed up again in something I read just yesterday. I love it!!

So, for yourself and for those to come, find your courage and go for it. You are far greater than you have ever imagined. Leave the metaphysical farm of your untrue thoughts planted in inflexible rows and, as Rosalind Russell said to her nephew in "Auntie Mame"—"Go! Live! You are magnificent!"

BREAKING FREE—
THEN WHAT?

꧁

F or much of my life, in spite of all the really good things
that have happened, I kept myself guarded from what I
perceived to be the consequences of opening up and being
fully me. This came about from my believing certain things
expressed either directly to me, or overheard in various
conversations throughout my growing up years. Things
like: "Why would you go to college when you will just end
up being married and raising kids anyway"—"It's ok to be
smart, but don't let it show too much because men don't
like that"—"Good Christian women don't dance and show
off and they especially don't get into theater because they
will be led astray"—"Too tall to be an airline hostess"—"You
are really brave to wear high heels. Hope you can find a tall
husband"—"You are strong and very creative, but that can
be intimidating to people, especially men"—"Go for it—but
be ready for disappointment," " You seemed so grown up
all the time and we didn't know what to do with you" and
other phrases that have stuck in my head.

These fueled my introverted tendencies and squelched
my extroverted ones. It also created some residual sadness
that still sits opposite the larger corner of the joy that has
always been alive in my heart. That sadness still wants to

show up once in a while. Perhaps some of you have experienced similar things.

Now, at this more advanced stage in my life questions like "How well do we really know ourselves?" and "How well do we really know what life is?" are still basically unanswered. That may not be what you wanted to hear, but it is the truth for me. I say that because life is still a mystery for me. It has given me so much along the way and I am richly blessed by everything. I could not have asked for more beautiful components in the various stages. But now the years ahead are mine to design.

I am freer now than I have ever been to be open to what is mine to receive, but I can honestly say that the space before me is much more unsettled than I thought it would be. At times it is just plain frightening. How does one dance that dance, sing that song, travel to those desired places, write that book, find love again, and make a final and meaningful contribution to the world? Maybe you know. I don't.

Some of you may be wanting, right now, to share your knowledge about the power of prayer, of affirmations, of faith, of hope, of keeping on keeping on, of trust in a higher power and the knowing that all is well; these things I share from the platform in my ministerial role. My self-talk is full of all of these because my belief in a higher power has never wavered. That is the Source to which I turn to each morning and each night. That is the One Power that will always rule my life. Yet, though it comforts me every step of the way and allows me to sleep well and function each day, it does not keep me from being human. My human part does not know how to do the next step and is asking "now what?" Now that I am, once again, totally free, how do I live my life?

IN HONOR OF COURAGE

꧁

The photo was of a blue pad supporting a mesh-covered head with dark open eye holes showing and tubes connecting to some sort of machines. The head was attached to a white t-shirted upper torso that belonged to the apparently well-muscled and strong body of a young man. All looked like something out of a science fiction movie where some inhabitants of an alien culture might be creating, and then producing, a form that would serve whatever purpose they had in mind. It certainly didn't look earth-like, especially with the small tube protruding from the mouth hole of the snuggly fitted mask. I winced when I saw it and felt the hot tears begin to stream down my face and for a moment I was in denial that this could be occurring.

This was a photo of my son, my beautiful, grown-up baby boy, receiving radiation for a cancerous intruder in his neck. A foreign-to-the-body, alien intrusion into healthy tissues to establish its own domain was meeting its destroyer with hopefully the right outcome that would return health to the still young, though mature body of a vibrant husband and father of five. The outcome was uncertain at that time, but hopes were high and prayers floated around the universe in affirmation that healing was not only possible, but on its way once the body began to respond by eradicating the tumor and rebuilding healthy tissue.

As I looked at the photo, many memories came back to me, like they do to all parents at one time or another throughout the years. I say big brown eyes, impetuous grin, features and body type so like his father's that made it looked like we had Xeroxed him on a copy machine and watched him become a full-blown body that we carried home from the hospital in a blue blanket, only to continue to be a somewhat mirror-like image of his father even up to this day. This young person, with the olive toned skin had shown the world many different ways to interpret things— such as the many ways a swing set could be enjoyed. When first constructed and in place in our back yard, his sister and a neighbor boy did the usual and sat in the swings. But, not my son. He immediately climbed to the top and sat on the bar, calling out to the world, "You can see everything from up here." That became a favorite perch, though he did occasionally use the seats for swinging, laying over them on his stomach, or standing up on them while in motion. Always finding a different way to do things and giving us some moments of real concern for safety.

Like his father, he did not know a stranger. Everyone he met was a potential friend, someone to play with, and in adult years he never lacked for friends. Preferring to make his musical presence known, he chose the drums over all other instruments. For profession, true to his preference for seeing things from higher up, he chose the top of airport towers to use his skills as an air-traffic controller. But now, his focus was inner, his world slowed down by the narrowing of the parameters of his days and nights. He was walking through a time of shadow, and he was walking it alone because, though they loved and supported him, his family could not be physically by his side. They were taking care of necessary business in another state during his transfer to the present location.

I am choosing at this time to honor my son for his courage, not only in the situation described here, but in all the areas of his life and career that have found him in many places, some truly in harm's way, many that required him being away from family, and some that did not. His support system was amazing, yet learning how to navigate through all of those instances produced a man of substance for which I will ever be proud. Like his sister, who has faced unbelievable challenges in her life as well, he has—and the two of them together have been angels in my life and I take great pride in their being-ness. The Spirit that encompasses all of life and through grace brings us home to our hearts, ourselves and life's meaning is present in them both. Right now I am imagining that the green light on the machine in use in the photo of the radiation treatment is a symbol of that Presence and am knowing, in my heart that no matter what, all is well and all will be well. I grieve for and with all those parents who have lost children, I pray for all the new lives coming into this experience, and give thanks for being given the chance to experience life.

Be well, my son. Be happy. Be well, my daughter. Be happy. You are both loved beyond measure.

About the Author

Sherry Lady was born and raised in Oregon. After receiving her BS degree from what was then Oregon College of Education, she spent 30 years as an elementary teacher. Four of those years were spent at The American School in Japan near Tokyo. Her husband taught at the high school and her children attended the elementary school. She received her Masters in Education from the University of Oregon. She also did post graduate work in theater at the U of O and Lane Community College. After retirement she attended ministerial school and was ordained in 1996. Since then she has served on the ministerial team at Unity of the Valley church in Eugene, Oregon. She has two children, eleven grandchildren and three great grandchildren. She loves travel, music, writing, theater, being in nature and celebrating life in every possible moment.

Julie Lady Hall is the author's daughter. She was born and raised in Oregon. She received her undergraduate degree from Luther College in Decorah, Iowa and her Masters in Education degree from the University of Central Florida. A former classroom teacher, she is now completing her Doctorate in Psychology. She enjoys, music, travel, writing and photography. She lives in Florida near her six children and one grandchild.

9 781643 886695